FINDING REFUGE IN CANADA

FINDING

REFUGE

IN

CANADA

narratives of dislocation

EDITED BY

GEORGE MELNYK & CHRISTINA PARKER

◊ AU PRESS

Copyright © 2021 George Melnyk and Christina Parker
Published by AU Press, Athabasca University
1200, 10011 – 109 Street, Edmonton, AB T5J 3S8

https://doi.org/10.15215/aupress/9781771993012.01

Cover design by Natalie Olsen
Interior design by Sergiy Kozakov
Printed and bound in Canada

Library and Archives Canada Cataloguing in Publication
Title: Finding refuge in Canada : narratives of dislocation / edited by George
    Melnyk and Christina Parker.
Names: Melnyk, George, editor. | Parker, Christina, editor.
Series: Global peace studies series.
Description: Series statement: Global peace studies series | Includes
    bibliographical references.
Identifiers: Canadiana (print) 20200409735 | Canadiana (ebook) 20200409832 |
    ISBN 9781771993012 (softcover) | ISBN 9781771993029 (PDF) |
    ISBN 9781771993036 (EPUB) | ISBN 9781771993043 (Kindle)
Subjects: LCSH: Refugees—Canada.
Classification: LCC HV640.4.C3 F56 2021 | DDC 362.870971—dc23

We acknowledge the financial support of the Government of Canada through
the Canada Book Fund (CBF) for our publishing activities and the assistance
provided by the Government of Alberta through the Alberta Media Fund.

Canadä   Alberta
                Government

Contents

Acknowledgements

The editors would like to thank the contributors for their willingness to share their personal stories with the public. Without these stories being made public the history of the refugee experience and those who helped them would have been lessened. We also appreciate the analysts of the refugee system in Canada for their thoughtful research and writing from which we learned so much. We would also like to thank the anonymous reviewers of the manuscript for their useful advice on improvements. We hope that in following their comments we enhanced the reading experience, increased accuracy, and provided a balanced perspective on the refugee experience. We are grateful for Athabasca University Press and their support in publishing this book. Notably, Pamela Holway and Karyn Wisselink were instrumental in making this collection a success. We also appreciate the thoughtful and thorough copyediting completed by Peter Midgley. Finally, we thank our spouses, Julia Melnyk and Vinay Shandal, for their patience throughout the process of putting this collection together.

FINDING

REFUGE

IN

CANADA

Refugees and Canada

Contemporary Issues and Real Stories

GEORGE MELNYK and CHRISTINA PARKER

No one chooses to become a refugee. It is a condition forced on people—by warfare; by political, religious, and gender-based persecution; by ethnic cleansing; by persistent violations of basic human rights; or, increasingly, by the environmental consequences of climate change. As many Canadians are aware, the world's refugee population has risen sharply over the past decade. By the end of 2019, the figure stood at 33.8 million, only a few million shy of the entire population of Canada. According to the office of the United Nations High Commissioner for Refugees (UNHCR), of these 33.8 million individuals who had fled their homelands, 26.0 million were "refugees" as defined by the United Nations, while the remainder were either asylum seekers (4.2 million) or displaced Venezuelans (3.6 million). Added to these were another 45.7 million internally displaced persons, who make up the remainder of the 79.5 million forcibly displaced persons worldwide—that is, one out of every 97 people (UNHCR 2020, 2, 8). Although these are staggering numbers, the total number of refugees that are resettled in other countries is about 0.4 percent, or about 100,000 annually (UNHCR 2020, 8). Despite these relatively low resettlement figures, the world has seen a surge of anti-refugee and anti-migrant in various developed nations.

Because the rhetoric of fear of "the other" is powerful, the language and actions of those who resist that rhetoric need to match that vehemence. This is especially important in Canada, a country that takes pride in its current reputation for compassion and inclusion. Historically, worries about uncontrolled immigration have been fanned from time to time by media and political leaders. These attitudes have defined Canada as much as the current mythology of openness has. This book questions to what extent Canada deserves a benign and welcoming reputation. As research suggests, whether Canadian government policy has been as humanitarian as people tend to assume is a matter of debate. In hopes of shedding additional light on this question, this book offers a series of first-person narratives written by refugees themselves and by people who work with them. These are stories from the frontlines written by people with direct experience of Canadian policies and procedures. The conflicting emotions that refugees experience, together with the sometimes troubling insights from those who provide support, can help us to understand what Canada does well and what it doesn't.

WHERE WE STAND TODAY

Like most countries, Canada does not accept limitless numbers of refugees each year. Rather, Immigration, Refugees and Citizenship Canada (IRCC) sets annual immigration targets, which include figures both for refugees resettled from abroad and for asylum seekers ("protected persons"), as well as for the number of new residents who will be admitted on humanitarian and compassionate grounds. According to targets set in the fall of 2018 (IRCC 2018), Canada's goal was to admit 31,700 resettled refugees in 2020—although the government would cover the cost of only 10,700 of these refugees, while the other two-thirds (21,000) would be privately sponsored refugees.[1] In contrast, the Canadian Council for Refugees was calling for a target of 20,000 government-assisted refugees (see CCR 2018), almost

---

1 The figure of 21,000 includes 1,000 refugees to be admitted under the government's PVOR (blended visa office-referred) program. Whereas private sponsors are ordinarily responsible for the financial support of refugees for an entire year, through the PVOR program, the government offers to cover the cost for a maximum of six months. For more information, see "Blended Visa Office-Referred Program: About the Process," Government of Canada, last modified March 3, 2018, https://www.canada.ca/en/immigration-refugees-citizenship/services/refugees/help-outside-canada/private-sponsorship-program/blended-visa-office-program.html.

twice the IRCC figure for 2020. In addition to these resettled refugees, IRCC set a target for the admission of 18,000 "protected persons" in 2020—that is, asylum seekers whose claims have been accepted by the Immigration and Refugee Board (IRB) (IRCC 2018). In its 2019–20 departmental plan, however, the IRB noted that "an inventory of more than 75,000 claims has accumulated, representing more than two years of work at current funding levels" (IRB 2019, 4). Even if only half the existing claims (37,500) are eventually accepted, at a maximum of 18,000 admissions per year, clearing this backlog effectively renders it impossible to accept any new claimants for at least two years.

Although the backlog had been building up for some time, much of it accumulated in the wake of the US presidential election in November 2016. The arrival in office of Donald Trump sparked a sudden upsurge in what the IRB terms "irregular border crossers," that is, asylum seekers who enter Canada from the United States without going through an official port of entry, usually with the intention of making a claim for refugee status once they are safely inside Canada. These new claimants had little choice but to cross the border "irregularly." Had they instead attempted to cross into Canada at an official entry point and claim refugee status at that time, they probably would have been turned back in accordance with the Canada–United States Safe Third Country Agreement, which requires asylum seekers to make their claim in the United States if they arrive there first, on the presumption that the United States is already a safe haven. Many of these border crossers are originally from countries such Haiti, Syria, Nepal, Somalia, and Yemen, whose citizens have temporary protected status in the United States. However, in light of the harsh attitudes toward "illegal aliens" promoted by President Trump, in tandem with his efforts to withdraw protected status for citizens of certain countries, these asylum seekers fear deportation, and so they attempt to find a more reliable place of safety in Canada (Chiasson 2018).[2]

In addition to these 31,700 resettled refugees, IRCC was planning to admit 4,500 persons on humanitarian and compassionate grounds in 2020.

2 In July 2017, this situation prompted the Canadian Council for Refugees, Amnesty International, and the Canadian Council of Churches to challenge whether the United States can reasonably be designated a safe third country for all refugees ("Legal Challenge of Safe Third Country Agreement Launched," July 5, 2017, Canadian Council for Refugees, https://ccrweb.ca/en/media/

From early 2017 through June 2020, the IRB received nearly 60,000 claims from "irregular" border crossers, of which roughly half were still pending at the end of this period. In the first three months of 2020 alone, the IRB received close to 3,500 new claims, although, in the following three months (April to June), the number plummeted by almost 90 percent as the COVID-19 pandemic set in.[3] In mid-March, the Canada-US border was closed to non-essential travel, and IRCC suspended refugee settlement operations, leaving many privately sponsored refugees stranded (see Ilcan 2020). At the same time, the government announced that, for the duration of the crisis, it would no longer accept refugee claims from irregular border crossers, who would instead be sent back to the United States (Austen 2020). The situation provoked outcry from refugee advocacy organizations on the grounds that Canada has a legal obligation not to turn refugees away (see Coletta 2020; Dickson 2020).

These asylum seekers "are not trying to sneak into Canada undetected," writes refugee law scholar Sean Rehaag (2019). They are simply trying to avoid immediate deportation back to the United States—the probable outcome were they to present themselves at a regular border station. Once across the border, they generally seek out Canadian authorities in order to make a refugee claim. Yet these border crossers have often been portrayed in the media as "queue jumpers" who are trying to bypass the standard refugee application procedure. In the imagination of some Canadians, they have come to symbolize the feared Other that political leaders in many countries have been railing against. Despite their relatively small numbers, these "irregular" arrivals have heightened anxiety and concern about Canada being "flooded" by unwanted people who might "steal jobs," or increase the taxpayer's burden, or dilute the national identity (Bryden 2018; Vomiero and Russell 2019). The fact is that Canada has accepted more than a million refugees over

---

legal-challenge-safe-third-country). In July 2020, the Federal Court determined that it cannot: the court ruled that that the agreement violates section 7 of the Canadian Charter of Rights and Freedoms, which guarantees the right to life, liberty, and personal security. The federal government is appealing the decision, and the agreement remains in force until the appeal is heard.

3 "Irregular Border Crosser Statistics," Immigration and Refugee Board of Canada, last modified September 9, 2020, https://irb-cisr.gc.ca/en/statistics/Pages/Irregular-border-crosser-statistics.aspx.

the past four decades, without any significant social or economic disruption. But, for some Canadians, the fear remains.

In contrast to the suspicious and even openly hostile reception given to irregular border crossers, Canadians extended a warm welcome to the resettled Syrian refugees who arrived in 2015–16, in flight from a country where war has claimed hundreds of thousands of lives. A survey conducted in October and November 2017 revealed that 7 percent of the respondents had been directly involved in the Syrian refugee sponsorship program, while an additional 25 percent indicated that they knew someone who had (Environics Institute 2018, 35; see also Adams 2018).[4] Such figures suggest a caring nation whose citizens reach out to those in crisis in other parts of the world, but these figures need to be contrasted with the situation of refugee claimants here in this country. Partly in consequence of the unanticipated increase in those fleeing the United States, the number of refugee claimants using homeless shelters in Toronto rose from 459 in late 2016 to 2,351 in April 2018, prompting Toronto's mayor, John Tory, to renew calls to the federal government for aid. Only days earlier, the Québec government had announced that Montréal's shelters were approaching capacity and would no longer accept refugee claimants. Tory was quoted as saying that, despite previous pleas for help with resettlement costs, no "meaningful co-ordinated response" had been forthcoming from Ottawa (Gray 2018).

Tory, who was among those who had helped to sponsor a Syrian family, went on to note that Canadians have a "moral responsibility to support refugees from around the world in their time of need" (quoted in Gray 2018). The moral responsibility he refers to should not apply solely to refugees abroad who have already passed government inspection, but to those who, out of fear for their safety, seek asylum in Canada at irregular border crossings. The current backlog of refugee claims means that asylum seekers may have to wait up to two years to have their cases heard. During that time, they may, if they are lucky, have the opportunity to take classes in English or French, to find a job, or to pursue an education, which would give them a head start

---

4 A total of 1,501 people (a "representative sample," according to Environics) took part in the survey (Environics Institute 2018, 1). A subsequent Environics survey, conducted in October 2019 as part of the institute's ongoing "Focus Canada" series, examined attitudes toward refugees in general and found that, while 43 percent of respondents disagreed with the statement "Most people claiming to be refugees are not real refugees," 39 percent agreed (Environics Institute 2019, 5).

should their claim be accepted. Then again, they may be left searching for a means to survive, as they await a verdict on their future.

A MIXED WELCOME: CANADA'S REFUGEE HISTORY

Canada's selective response to new arrivals has a long history, one that is all but inseparable from the project of nation building. This history is also one of immigration, given that, until the 1970s, Canada made no formal distinction between refugees and immigrants. As James Hathaway puts it, "What mattered was not the motive for immigration, but rather the immigrant's potential to contribute to the economic development of Canada" (1988, 679)—a principle that has continued to guide the country's policies, even with regard to some refugees.

In the latter part of the nineteenth century, Canada welcomed such diverse (and often small) groups as Jews fleeing pogroms in tsarist Russia and likewise the Doukhobors, who, as pacifists, refused to do military service and whose spirituality conflicted with Russian orthodoxy. Under the patronage of Count Leo Tolstoy, the Doukhobors migrated to Canada, where they became part of the influx of settlers into the newly opened West—an expansion predicated, of course, on the dispossession of Indigenous peoples.

During the early twentieth century, Canada became an increasingly xenophobic nation, primarily in view of the arrival, over the previous two decades, of large numbers of immigrants from places other than Britain and northern Europe. At the time many Anglo-Canadians interested in establishing their powerful position as occupants and owners of Canada were alarmed by the influx of immigrants from southern and eastern Europe, who were considered inferior because of their culture, language, religion, and mores. There was a widespread attitude that these immigrants could either not assimilate or, if they did, might dilute the national identity. Anglo-Canadian settlers reacted in part by embracing racist ideas drawn from social Darwinism and theories of eugenics, and the desire to ensure that Canada would remain a white country was reflected in immigration policy. In response to public pressure, the Immigration Act was amended in 1906 and again in 1910 "to provide for greater selectivity in the admissions process in order to weed out undesirable immigrants." In addition, "Cabinet was given enhanced powers to exclude any class of immigrant where it deemed such exclusion to be in the best interests of the country" (Kelley and Trebilcock 1998, 14–15).

In a now infamous episode, which occurred in 1914, port authorities in Vancouver refused to allow a ship containing several hundred Punjabis (most of them Sikhs) to land. As Sarah Wallace points out, the incident took place in the context of widespread but unsubstantiated fears that people from South Asia were carriers of disease and hence "not fit to stay." Ultimately, the SS *Komagata Maru* was forced to return to India. Although these would-be immigrants had not started out as refugees, they were greeted with hostility by the British upon their arrival in Calcutta. When officials attempted to arrest one of the passengers, twenty died in an initial skirmish with British troops, and most were imprisoned while an inquiry was conducted (see Wallace 2017, 140–47).

During World War I, Canada incarcerated thousands of "enemy aliens," many of whom were non-Germanic people from the Austro-Hungarian Empire, including a great many Ukrainians. Then, in 1919, Canada banned further immigration of Doukhobors, Hutterites, and Mennonites. It was three years before Mennonite leaders were able to convince the federal government to lift the ban. By the end of the decade, approximately twenty thousand Russian Mennonites—refugees from religious persecution in the Soviet Union—had arrived in Canada. Most were farmers, and, because of their agricultural background, they settled chiefly in southern Ontario and western Canada. During the 1930s, however, official immigration dwindled to a mere trickle, given the high levels of unemployment during the Great Depression.

During World War II, Canada adopted a notably unwelcoming attitude toward Jewish refugees from the Holocaust. In 1939 Canada joined the United States and Cuba in refusing sanctuary to more than nine hundred Jews in flight from Nazi Germany aboard the MS *St. Louis*. Its passengers, bound for the United States via Cuba, were not permitted to disembark in Havana and were also denied entry into the United States. When the Canadian government learned of the situation, it followed suit. The *St. Louis* had no choice but to return to Europe, where over a quarter of its passengers ultimately perished in concentration camps. In the twelve-year period from 1933 to 1945, Canada admitted fewer than five thousand Jews—a record that has been described as "arguably the worst of all possible refugee-receiving states" (Abella and Troper 1986, xxii; see also 63–66). In November 2018, Prime Minister Justin Trudeau formally apologized for Canada's actions with regard to the *St. Louis* (just as he had done in May 2016 for the *Komagata Maru* incident).[5]

After World War II, Europe—now divided into a Soviet-controlled East and an Allied-control West—was awash with displaced people. Many of those displaced came to Canada, where they fuelled the postwar economy. As Hathaway points out, the Canadian government "maintained its focus on domestic economic interests by specifically seeking out the most 'adaptable' European refugees from among those in need of resettlement" (1988, 680), even as it was painting its actions as humanitarian. In addition, during the Cold War of the 1950s and 1960s, Canada showed a preference for refugees whose ideological sympathies aligned with its own, admitting thousands of anti-Communist refugees from the failed Hungarian uprising of 1956 and then doing the same after the revolt in Czechoslovakia in 1968.

The first non-white refugees admitted to Canada in large numbers were South Asian Ismaili Muslims who were driven out of Uganda in 1972. Shortly afterwards, Chileans fleeing the coup in Chile in 1973 were admitted to Canada, the first time the country had welcomed politically left-wing groups of refugees. By the end of the decade, Canada began admitting refugees from Vietnam and then from Cambodia and Laos as well. This broadening of immigration horizons was facilitated by the formal elimination in 1962 of the overtly discriminatory language that had, until then, characterized its immigration policies, including the infamous Chinese head tax in force from the late nineteenth century until just after World War II. In 1967, revised immigration regulations instituted a point system that, in theory, did not discriminate on the basis of nationality or race but instead evaluated potential immigrants primarily in terms of their skills, their level of education, their ability to speak English or French, and their family connections (if any) within Canada. While there may not be a point system specifically for use with refugees, the government does have to decide which refugees to accept for resettlement in Canada. When it comes to making these choices,

5 For these apologies, see "Statement by the Prime Minister on the Anniversary of the *Komagata Maru* Incident," May 23, 2016, https://pm.gc.ca/eng/news/2018/05/23/statement-prime-minister-anniversary-komagata-maru-incident; and "Statement of Apology on Behalf of the Government of Canada to the Passengers of the MS *St. Louis*," November 7, 2018, https://pm.gc.ca/en/news/speeches/2018/11/07/statement-apology-behalf-government-canada-passengers-ms-st-louis.

there may be an underlying predilection for young, educated, and/or skilled refugees, in accordance with the point system's emphasis on potential economic benefit to Canada.

THE CANADIAN REFUGEE SYSTEM

Until the early 1970s, Canada had no legal structures in place for dealing specifically with refugees. Although a beginning was made in 1973, with amendments to the Immigration Appeal Board Act, a formal system for admitting refugees was first laid out in the Immigration Act of 1976. Since then, the Canadian system for accepting refugees has continued to evolve in response to shifts in the political climate at home as well as developments abroad that have given rise to an ever-growing number of people seeking asylum. The admission of refugees to Canada is currently regulated under the Immigration and Refugee Protection Act, which went into effect in 2002.

While it is possible to apply for refugee status from within Canada, most of the refugees who come to Canada have been granted asylum while still resident abroad. The Canadian government issues visas to refugees who have been vetted and whose total number corresponds to annual targets. In most cases, these resettled refugees have been recognized by UNHCR Canada as "Convention" refugees—that is, refugees as defined in the 1951 United Nations Convention Relating to the Status of Refugees (which Canada signed only in 1969). Inland applicants, that is, those who apply for refugee status from within Canada, are evaluated through a process known as the refugee determination system, which is administered through the IRB. The IRB was established in 1989, when legislation introduced in 1987 by the Brian Mulroney government went into effect.[6] The IRB adjudicates claims from individuals who have entered the country by standard legal means (for example, on student visas or as tourists) and subsequently made application for asylum. It also adjudicates the claims of those who entered the country "irregularly," whether by walking across the border from the United States or by arriving on Canada's shores by sea.

In 2012, the Protecting Canada's Immigration System Act effected significant changes to Canada's refugee determination system. These changes

---

6 This legislation generated considerable controversy. See the discussion in Hathaway (1988, 703–8), as well as his follow-up article (Hathaway 1989). See also the chapter by William Janzen in this volume.

elicited strenuous criticisms from human rights organizations, including the Canadian Civil Liberties Association, Human Rights Watch, and Amnesty International. Critics pointed to unreasonable timelines: under the revised law, newly arrived refugees have only two weeks to file a claim, and a hearing must take place within 60 days—hardly enough time for an applicant to assemble adequate documentation. In addition, the rights of refugees from "designated countries of origin" (that is, countries regarded as "safe") have been seriously curtailed. Timelines are even shorter, and, if rejected, these claimants are unable to appeal to the IRB and may face immediate deportation, even if they have successfully applied to the Federal Court for a judicial review of their case. Such claimants must also wait a year before they can apply for compassionate and humanitarian consideration, during which time they may well be deported. Moreover, under the revised law, those designated as "irregular arrivals" by the Minister of Public Safety are subject to mandatory detention if they are sixteen or older, and they have no right of appeal. If their claim for refugee status is ultimately accepted, they cannot apply for permanent resident status for at least five years, making it impossible for spouses and children who are still abroad to join them in Canada.[7] All in all, such policies do not align very well with Canada's image of itself as a welcoming country.

In the face of a growing backlog of refugee claims, the minister of Immigration, Refugees and Citizenship Canada launched an independent review of the IRB's asylum processing procedures in June 2017. The resulting report opened with a clear assessment of the current situation: "The refugee determination system is at a crossroads. Once again it is dealing with a surge in claims that it is ill-equipped to manage, running the risk of creating a large backlog that, if not tackled promptly, may take years to bring to final resolution" (Yeates 2018, 1). The report recommended several measures that would streamline operations. Yet, as refugee policy analyst Robert Falconer pointed out in November 2019, "Despite these attempts at procedural reform, the number of claims processed by the IRB has continued to drop since peaking

7 For a useful summary of these criticisms, see "Concerns About Changes to the Refugee Determination System," Canadian Council for Refugees, December 2012, https://ccrweb.ca/en/concerns-changes-refugee-determinatio n-system. See also "Canada: Vote No on Migrant Detention Bill," Human Rights Watch, March 16, 2012, https://www.hrw.org/news/2012/03/16/ canada-vote-no-on-migrant-detention-bill.

in March 2019." By the end of September 2019, Falconer noted—a month in which 5,560 new claims were made but fewer than 2,880 processed—the number of unprocessed claims had reached 82,240 (Falconer 2019).

The delays take an enormous human toll. Even if refugee claimants are not held temporarily in a detention centre or threatened with immediate deportation, they face what must seem like an interminable wait for a decision on their case. This produces not relief but renewed psychological strain, as claimants struggle to adapt to life in Canada while living with the possibility that they will ultimately be forced to leave. In short, while the current system may appear on the surface to be respectful of human rights and of Canada's commitments under the UN Refugee Convention, the refugee determination process is still vulnerable to massive overload, with little by way of a solution in sight.

It is, moreover, susceptible to abuse. According to an IRCC backgrounder, "All eligible refugee claimants receive a fair hearing at the IRB, an independent, quasi-judicial tribunal. Each case is decided on its merits, based on the evidence and arguments presented" (IRCC 2017). Yet over roughly the past decade, several researchers have called the fairness of the refugee determination system into question. Although IRCC's reference to "evidence and arguments" clearly aims to suggest a rational and objective process, research conducted by Sean Rehaag has uncovered a subjective dimension to the review system. Examining data for 2017, Rehaag found vast disparities in refugee claim recognition rates across decision makers, with some adjudicators accepting nearly all the claims they reviewed and others accepting fewer than one in four. This variation, Rehaag says, is consistent with findings from earlier years, both before and after the revisions contained in Protecting Canada's Immigration System Act. In Rehaag's estimation, "The persistence of unexplained variations in recognition rates across adjudicators in the new refugee determination system, combined with the devastating potential impact of false negative refugee decisions (i.e., refugees being returned to face persecution), make robust oversight mechanisms essential" (Rehaag 2018a).

But the issue of variance does not just involve adjudicators. It also involves Federal Court judges who preside over applications by refugees for a judicial review of the adjudicator's decision. A separate study of judicial review determinations prompted Rehaag to conclude that an applicant's chances of success depended in large measure on the judge, with one judge approving fewer than 1.5 percent of the applications considered and another approving nearly 78 percent (Rehaag 2012, 25). As Rehaag notes, these are high-stakes decisions, given that "if the Federal Court wrongly denies applications, the direct result is that refugees may, contrary to international refugee law, be sent back to countries where they face persecution, torture or death" (31). A follow-up study, which included data that postdated the 2012 revisions to the determination system, identified a similar pattern, prompting Rehaag to conclude that "refugee claimants whose applications for judicial review are denied continue to have good reason to wonder whether this was because of the facts of their case and the law, or whether they simply lost the luck of the draw" (2018b, 17).

An important factor in each case before the IRB is the credibility of the oral story of the claimant, especially when written documentation is limited. These oral accounts rely, of course, on memory, and, as Hilary Evans Cameron has pointed out, when claimants' stories vary even slightly from time to time, decision makers tend to become distrustful. While acknowledging that in some cases gaps or inconsistencies in a claimant's testimony may rightly undermine its credibility, she argues that such lapses are often misleading and "should never be used mechanically" (2010, 469). In her analysis, adjudicators—whose assumptions and perceptions are influenced by their Canadian training and perspective—often misconceive how memory operates, especially in stressful situations such as the IRB proceedings. Applicants who speak through interpreters are not only nervous about their applications and the formality of the proceedings but may still be dealing with past trauma. As a result, they can easily become confused or uncertain and so appear evasive or untruthful. These factors can be prejudicial to asylum seekers when the culturally biased and bureaucratic standards of authenticity that adjudicators bring to the cases result in applicants being judged unreliable or untruthful. As Evans Cameron concludes, "Many decision makers must fundamentally readjust their thinking about claimants' memories if they are to avoid making findings that are as unsound as they are unjust" (469).

Concerns have also been raised about the increased use of detention by the Canada Border Services Agency (CBSA) in recent years, enabled by the reforms of 2012. Not surprisingly, the IRCC website has little to say about detention, although the backgrounder they provide does offer a brief explanation: "People who are intercepted by the RCMP or local law enforcement after crossing the border irregularly are brought to the nearest CBSA port of entry or inland CBSA or IRCC office (whichever is closest), where an officer will conduct an immigration examination, including considering whether detention is warranted" (IRCC 2017). According to researcher-advocates Petra Molnar and Stephanie Silverman, the CBSA detained an average of 7,215 individuals per year in the period from 2012 to 2017, each of whom spent, on average, 19.5 days behind bars. Moreover, because parents who are placed in detention must decide "whether their children should be 'housed' with them or placed in foster care," Canada does—despite claims to the contrary—detain children (Molnar and Silverman 2018b). The CBSA has acknowledged that, in 2017, 151 minors were held in custody with parents, and an additional eleven were detained unaccompanied by an adult (Shingler 2018).

In response to widespread criticisms, the government has professed concern about its detention system, yet little appears to have changed. In August 2016, Molnar and Silverman wrote: "Under international law, detention should be a measure of last resort. It should be non-punitive, non-arbitrary, and conducted with regard to due process, and must not sweep up asylum seekers or other vulnerable people. Unfortunately, this is not always the case in Canada" (Molnar and Silverman 2016). Their comments came on the eve of an announcement by Canada's Minister of Public Safety—the minister responsible for the CBSA—of the government's intention to upgrade its immigration detention centres and to increase the availability of alternatives to detention (CBC News 2018). In April 2018, Molnar and Silverman wrote: "The Canadian immigration detention regime is rife with violence, distress and despair. Detainees are separated from their families, denied access to legal counsel, faced with the removal of their kids and imprisoned in far-flung locations with little access to psycho-social supports and medical care" (Molnar and Silverman 2018a).

Delphine Nakache has drawn attention to another very troubling aspect of the use of detention—namely, the parallel it draws between asylum seekers and criminals. This parallel is thrown into high relief when, as is not uncommon, would-be refugees are housed in provincial prisons, rather than in immigration detention facilities. As Nakache observes, the incarceration of refugee claimants serves to segregate them from the surrounding social space. Prisons thus come to function in much the same way as internment camps, marking asylum seekers as "undesirables" (Nakache 2013, 100). Indeed, the criminalization of those seeking asylum—that is to say, the assumption that if they have crossed the border illegally they must be, by nature, criminals—is necessary to justify the application of punitive measures.

Given that Canada does not sit on the border of one of the world's many conflict zones, its system is not equipped to cope with large numbers of asylum seekers. But there is another factor at work in Canada's approach to refugees. As Hathaway writes, "refugees were admitted as part of the general immigration scheme, which was designed to promote domestic economic interests"—a circumstance that "has conditioned much of the modern legal evolution in the field of Canadian refugee protection" (1988, 680). This tendency to view refugees as a subset of immigrants is still in evidence today, both in government policy and in the public mind. In selecting refugees from abroad, the government still aims to balance humanitarian concerns with pragmatic considerations, including the country's economic welfare, while complaints about border crossers often focus on potential competition for jobs.

The uncritical equation of refugees and immigrants is not only false but damaging, as it insidiously shifts the emphasis from humanitarian obligation to matters of economic benefit. Unlike immigrants seeking opportunities for a better future, refugees have been forcibly displaced. Many have been subjected to violence and have lived in fear of death—their own and/or that of immediate family members. Very frequently, refugees are suffering the effects of trauma. While escaping from a war zone or a refugee camp is no doubt a relief, they find themselves in an unfamiliar culture, surrounded by people speaking a language that may be entirely unknown to them, as they attempt to find housing and work. The scale of the disorientation can be overwhelming, and when we confuse immigrants with refugees, we risk losing sight of the conditions under which refugees arrive in Canada. This book aims to make these distinctions visible.

WHAT REFUGEE NARRATIVES TEACH US

In one way or another, the stories in this book are about self-transformation. Becoming a refugee means starting over: it means leaving behind one life and building a new one. Having to start over, often from a social, career, and financial position way below what refugees were accustomed to in their previous homeland, has been known to lead to mental health implications and distress (Beiser and Hou 2006; Hilario et al. 2018). But, as the narratives written by those who work or have worked with refugees suggest, supporting a refugee through this process is also transforming. It is difficult to help someone without becoming emotionally engaged in their experience, which then becomes part of one's own experience. This sense of new beginnings lends a positive tone to these narratives. The contributors to this volume are understandably proud of what they have accomplished, whether in terms of adjusting to life in Canada or of making it possible for others to do so. Yet these stories also touch on the frustrations, the disappointments, and the deficiencies that mar Canada's refugee acceptance system. While none of those who volunteered to tell their story set out to complain or criticize, their accounts offer a revealing counterpoint to Canada's self-congratulatory image.

Several themes emerge in the narratives. One is the strain of adaptation to unfamiliar places, cultures, languages, and customs, and a concomitant sense of loss. Another is a sense of guilt, compounded by fears for those left behind. A third is the stigma associated with the refugee identity. Those who assist refugees speak of the obstacles posed by the bureaucratic process, about how they struggle to understand the situation those they are trying to support find themselves in, and of the personal rewards of seeing someone successfully adapt to life in Canada.

Victor Porter, whose political activity in Argentina ended in his imprisonment and torture, was ultimately able to escape to Canada as a government-sponsored refugee. But he is well aware that many others were not as fortunate, and he still regrets "the amount of pain and suffering that my detention caused to my parents and sister." Their anxiety over his fate was very high. Once in Canada, he also felt the strain of adaptation: "I struggled to learn English, to understand the country, and to find and make my way. I worked as a dishwasher, delivered newspapers, became a cook, a beekeeper, a production manager in the first tofu wiener factory in the country." In the end, he became an advocate for immigrants and refugees. The desire to give back is illustrated in other narratives as well. It is rooted in compassion, and yet it may also be a way of coping with a lingering sense of guilt, a feeling that those who were successful in finding a haven owe a debt to others.

Matida Daffeh, a human rights activist from The Gambia who came to Canada relatively recently, reiterates the theme of guilt. Daffeh was safe in Canada when she learned that her mother had passed away. "I thought of all the emotional trauma my mother had endured because of me," she writes, "and I began to tremble. I felt guilty and sad that I could not be there to mourn with the rest of the family." Not being able to share in a family's normal life detracts from one's sense of value and usefulness. The lack of freedom to travel to attend important family tragedies or milestones, and the resulting isolation, makes refugees feel both separated and imprisoned. Daffeh's experience also illustrates the daunting nature of the refugee determination process. Given its complexities (including the need to fill out lengthy forms in either English or French), those who have solid legal counsel throughout the process fare much better. Without such expert legal advice, Daffeh might have failed in her claim.

Boban Stojanović writes: "The moment my partner and I decided to leave our country was the moment we became tired." They were finally feeling the weariness of all those years of struggling for gay rights in Serbia, combined with the sense of exhaustion that comes from deciding to abandon a fight in hopes of a more peaceful existence. Stojanović applied for asylum after coming to Canada on a tourist visa, only to discover that, as a refugee, his life had become "one of lost privileges, limited rights, dependence on elementary things, and the inability to make any plan. Also, uncertainty." In Serbia, Stojanović and his partner knew who they were, but by making a refugee claim they had to surrender their former selves—all their familiar points of reference—and turn to face the very hard task of becoming someone new.

Flora Terah, a women's rights activist who fled to Canada for reasons of personal safety after her only child was murdered, was also obliged to start over, and she struggled to cope with the trauma she had endured. After coming to Canada, she tells us, "Even though I was enjoying people's concern for my welfare, my thoughts were fixed on Kenya, and grief was chewing at me. None of my hosts noticed that underneath my smile there was grief, worry, and pain." The pain in becoming a refugee involves not merely loss of place but loss of one's former sources of emotional support. "Fleeing Kenya," Terah writes, "had sucked a substantial amount of self-confidence and self-esteem out of me. I needed help." As her story illustrates, refugees may feel considerable, if unspoken, social pressure to keep negative emotions out of sight—given that, consciously or not, would-be rescuers generally expect those they have rescued to be grateful and happy. As a result, refugees often grapple in isolation with sorrow, doubt, and depression.

Depending on the circumstances, refugees may also be left with an abiding sense of shame. Cyrus Sundar Singh writes of the Sri Lankan Tamils who were found off the shores of Newfoundland in 1986, crowded together in two waterlogged lifeboats in which they had floated for three days in the North Atlantic. Although Canada allowed them to remain, they arrived to a mixed reception. Many ended up working in Toronto restaurants as cooks and in other low-waged positions, always remaining invisible, ashamed of their identity as "boat people." Here, we have a glimpse of the hierarchy that emerges among refugees. As we have seen, Canada has a distinct preference for "resettled" refugees who arrive in the country armed with an official welcome in the form of a visa issued abroad. Such refugees are a known quantity. "Irregular" arrivals are another matter, especially if they have little by way of education and skills. The Sri Lankan Tamils understood they had no invitation.

As many of these stories illustrate, refugees from countries in the Global South experience deeper forms of exclusion, owing to the persistence of racism in Canada. Stojanović, for instance, felt a greater sense of acceptance than, for example, did Terah. Although considerations of race or ethnicity have been officially expunged from Canadian immigration policy, they resurface in other criteria, such as level of education, fluency in English or French, and the ability of a new arrival to contribute to the economy. Likewise, refugees from countries whose nationals, either as immigrants or refugees, have established a strong presence in Canada have the advantage of advocacy by that group. Refugees from countries that do not have a previously established presence may face more difficulties because their support network is not yet established and they are more isolated.

As for those who tell the story of their assistance to refugees, we find there are both highs and lows. Mike Molloy, who worked on the front lines of the evacuation of South Asians from Uganda in the early 1970s, and William Janzen, of the Mennonite Central Committee, who contributed to the adoption of the ground-breaking policy on private sponsorship, both "feel privileged to have been involved with refugees," as Janzen puts it, confirming the theme of personal reward. Katharine Lake Berz and Julia Holland, who sponsored an illiterate Syrian refugee family in 2016, provide a telling account of their frustration with waiting for the bureaucratic process to provide their refugee family. "We waited for weeks, then months," they write. They asked themselves, "Were they ill and unable to travel? Had they decided against coming to Canada?" As sponsors, Lake Berz and Holland have learned that "refugees are not 'lucky.'" They may have escaped death and destruction, but they live "in constant fear for the safety of their friends and relatives." They fear they will never see them again.

Shelley Campagnola, who has worked a long time in the field, summarizes the overall situation this way:

> The asylum system itself is a complex one that mixes politics, policies of scrutiny and suspicion, public perceptions, and opinionated rhetoric with the personal pain of real people. It tries to bring justice while not upsetting local budgets, international relationships, economic trading partners, and voters who too often are ill-informed and easily inflamed by incomplete media reporting.

Campagnola's perspective on where Canada stands today is both accurate and insightful. For the most part, Canada has been insulated from major global flows of asylum seekers, and its asylum system is accustomed to dealing only with relatively small numbers. But forcible displacement is a growing phenomenon globally, and in many places the rhetoric of walls has sprung up in response. If, by contrast, Canada has so far been able to present itself as a model of tolerance, this is partly because numbers have remained low. How much longer this delicate balance can be maintained is anyone's guess. But by reminding us that refugees are human beings, not statistics, the stories in this book prepare us to respond with compassion to whatever lies ahead.

It is important to remember that this book is not intended to be all-inclusive. We recognize that this handful of stories cannot possibly capture the full spectrum of the refugee experience. With respect to the refugees themselves, our goal was to emphasize the individuality of each person's experience, which is inevitably influenced by factors such as gender, race, social and economic class, education, and language abilities, as well as the historical and cultural circumstances in which their migration occurred. Because we wished these voices to be heard without the mediation of a translator, we sought to identify contributors whose English was relatively fluent. It was unfortunately not feasible to include stories from people whose refugee claims were rejected, not only because such individuals can be hard to locate but also because some may still be in the process of appeal. We also wanted to highlight the variety of paths by which those who support refugees are led to their work. It is our hope that the voices presented in this text will spark deep reflection upon, dialogue with, and activism over how refugees are supported, integrated, and included in Canada.

WORKS CITED

Abella, Irving, and Harold Troper. 1986. *None Is Too Many: Canada and the Jews of Europe, 1933–1948*. Toronto: Lester and Orpen Dennys.

Adams, Michael. 2018. "Canada in 2018 Is a Country of Global Citizens." *Globe and Mail*, April 16, 2018. https://www.theglobeandmail.com/opinion/article-canada-in-2018-is-a-country-of-global-citizens/.

Aston, Perry. 2015. "What Is Canada Doing in Syria?" *Globe and Mail*, October 2, 2015. https://www.theglobeandmail.com/opinion/editorials/what-is-canada-doing-in-syria/article26634142/.

Austen, Ian. 2020. "In Shift, Trudeau Says Canada Will Return Asylum Seekers to U.S." *New York Times*, March 20, 2020. https://www.nytimes.com/2020/03/20/world/canada/trudeau-asylum-seekers-coronavirus.html.

Austin, Steve. 2013. "Crude Oil and the Syrian Conflict." *Oil-Price.net*, November 12, 2013. http://www.oil-price.net/en/articles/crude-oil-syrian-conflict.php.

Axworthy, Lloyd, and Allan Rock. 2018. "Let's Ensure Our Border Remains a Beacon of Hope." *Globe and Mail*, June 11, 2018. https://www.theglobeandmail.com/opinion/article-lets-ensure-our-border-remains-a-beacon-of-hope/.

Beiser, Morton, and Feng Hou. 2006. "Ethnic Identity, Resettlement Stress and Depressive Affect Among Southeast Asian Refugees in Canada." *Social Science and Medicine* 63, no. 1: 137–50.

Bryden, Joan. 2018. "Reality Check: Is Canada Facing an Asylum Seeker 'Crisis'?" *Global News*, August 16, 2018. https://globalnews.ca/news/4391589/asylum-seeker-crisis-canada/.

Canadian Press. 2018. "Canada to Increase Annual Immigration Admissions to 350,000 by 2021." *CBC News*, October 31, 2018. https://www.cbc.ca/news/politics/canada-immigration-increase-350000-1.4886546.

CBC News. 2018. "Canada's Immigration Detention Program to Get $138M Makeover." *CBC News*, August 15, 2018. https://www.cbc.ca/news/canada/montreal/goodale-immigration-laval-1.3721125.

CCR (Canadian Council for Refugees). 2018. "Low Number for Refugees Accepted in Canada Is a Serious Concern in Immigration Levels." Media release. November 2, 2018. https://ccrweb.ca/en/media/immigration-levels-accepted-refugees-permanent-residence.

Chiasson, Paul. 2018. "Federal Government Looks to Close Loophole That Encourages Irregular Border Crossings." *National Post*, April 18, 2018.

https://nationalpost.com/news/politics/budget-bill-would-tighten-loophole-that-encourages-irregular-border-crossing.

Coletta, Amanda. 2020. "Asylum Seekers Risk Their Lives to Help Canada Fight Covid-19." *Washington Post,* June 14, 2020. https://www.washingtonpost.com/world/the_americas/coronavirus-canada-asylum-seeker-nursing-home/2020/06/11/353b9756-abf0-11ea-a9d9-a81c1a491c52_story.html.

Dickson, Janice. 2020. "Four Asylum Seekers Turned Away at Canada-U.S. Border." *Globe and Mail,* April 5, 2020. https://www.theglobeandmail.com/politics/article-six-asylum-seekers-turned-away-at-canada-us-border/.

Environics Institute. 2018. *Canada's World Survey, 2018: Final Report.* April 2018. Toronto: Environics Institute for Survey Research. https://www.environicsinstitute.org/projects/project-details/canada%27s-world-2017-survey.

———. 2019. *Focus Canada—Fall 2019: Canadian Public Opinion About Immigration and Refugees.* Toronto: Environics Institute for Survey Research. https://www.environicsinstitute.org/projects/project-details/canadian-public-opinion-on-immigration-and-refugees.

Evans Cameron, Hilary. 2010. "Refugee Status Determinations and the Limits of Memory." *International Journal of Refugee Law* 22, no. 4: 469–511.

Falconer, Robert. 2019. "The Asylum Claim Backlog Surpasses 80,000 Cases." *Social Policy Trends,* November 2019. School of Public Policy, University of Calgary. https://www.policyschool.ca/wp-content/uploads/2019/11/Social-Policy-Trends-Asylum-Claim-Processing-November-2019.pdf.

Gray, Jeff. 2018. "Toronto Calls on Ottawa for Help in Handling Homeless Refugees." *Globe and Mail,* April 27, 2018. https://www.theglobeandmail.com/canada/toronto/article-toronto-calls-for-help-to-handle-refugees/.

Hathaway, James C. 1988. "Selective Concern: An Overview of Refugee Law in Canada." *McGill Law Journal* 33, no. 4: 676–715.

———. 1989. "Postscript—Selective Concern: An Overview of Refugee Law in Canada." *McGill Law Journal* 34, no. 2: 354–57.

Hilario, Carla T., John L. Oliffe, Josephine P. Wong, Annette J. Browne, and Joy L. Johnson. 2018. "'Just as Canadian as Anyone Else'? Experiences of Second-Class Citizenship and the Mental Health of Young Immigrant and Refugee Men in Canada." *American Journal of Men's Health* 12, no. 2: 210–20.

Ilcan, Suzan. 2020. "Re-bordering Canada's Privately Sponsored Refugees During the Pandemic." *openDemocracy,* June 15, 2020. https://www.opendemocracy.net/en/pandemic-border/re-bordering-canadas-privately-sponsored-refugees-during-the-pandemic/.

IRB (Immigration and Refugee Board of Canada). 2019. *2019–20 Departmental Plan.* Ottawa: Minister of Immigration, Refugees and Citizenship.

https://irb-cisr.gc.ca/en/reports-publications/planning-performance/
Documents/departmental-plan-report-1920.pdf.

IRCC (Immigration, Refugees and Citizenship Canada). 2017. "Claiming Asylum in Canada—What Happens?" Backgrounder. March 2, 2017. Last modified December 21, 2018. https://www.canada.ca/en/immigration-refugees-citizenship/news/2017/03/claiming_asylum_incanadawhathappens.html.

———. 2018. "Notice: Supplementary Information 2019–2021 Immigration Levels Plan." October 31, 2018. https://www.canada.ca/en/immigration-refugees-citizenship/news/notices/supplementary-immigration-levels-2019.html.

Kelley, Ninette, and Michael J. Trebilcock. 1998. *The Making of the Mosaic: A History of Canadian Immigration Policy.* Toronto: University of Toronto Press.

Molnar, Petra, and Stephanie J. Silverman. 2016. "Research Findings from Immigration Detention: Arguments for Increasing Access to Justice." *Canadian Association for Refugee and Forced Migration Studies* (blog), August 15, 2016. https://carfms.apps01.yorku.ca/blog/research-findings-from-immigration-detention-arguments-for-increasing-access-to-justice/.

———. 2018a. "How Canada's Immigration Detention System Spurs Violence Against Women." *The Conversation,* April 15, 2018. http://theconversation.com/how-canadas-immigration-detention-system-spurs-violence-against-women-95009.

———. 2018b. "Canada Needs to Get Out of the Immigration Detention Business." *CBC News,* July 5, 2018. https://www.cbc.ca/news/opinion/immigration-detention-1.4733897.

Nakache, Delphine. 2013. "Détention des demandeurs d'asile au Canada: Des logiques pénales et administratives convergentes." *Criminologie* 46, no. 1: 83–105. https://www.erudit.org/en/journals/crimino/2013-v46-n1-crimino0551/1015294ar/.

Rehaag, Sean. 2012. "Judicial Review of Refugee Determinations: The Luck of the Draw?" *Queen's Law Journal* 38, no. 1. http://dx.doi.org/10.2139/ssrn.2027517.

———. 2018a. "2017 Refugee Claim Data and IRB Member Recognition Rates." Canadian Council for Refugees. March 26, 2018. https://ccrweb.ca/en/2017-refugee-claim-data.

———. 2018b. "Judicial Review of Refugee Determinations (II): Revisiting the Luck of the Draw." Working paper, September 14, 2018. Forthcoming in *Queen's Law Journal.* http://dx.doi.org/10.2139/ssrn.3249723.

———. 2019. "Closing the Canada-U.S. Asylum Border Agreement Loophole? Not So Fast." *The Conversation,* March 25, 2019. http://theconversation.

com/closing-the-canada-u-s-asylum-border-agreement-loophole-not-so-
fast-114116.

Shingler, Benjamin. 2018. "Canada Aims to Avoid Detaining Migrant Children,
but It Happens." *CBC News*, June 20, 2018. https://www.cbc.ca/news/canada/
montreal/canada-detention-children-united-states-1.4709632.

Trudeau, Justin. 2016. "Statement by the Prime Minister on the Anniversary of
the Komagata Maru Incident." May 23, 2016. Ottawa. https://pm.gc.ca/eng/
news/2018/05/23/statement-prime-minister-anniversary-komagata-maru-
incident.

UNHCR (United Nations High Commissioner for Refugees). 2020. *Global
Trends: Forced Displacement in 2019*. Geneva: Office of the United Nations
High Commissioner for Refugees. https://www.unhcr.org/5ee200e37.pdf.

Vomiero, Jessica, and Andrew Russell. 2019. "Ipsos Poll Shows Canadians Have
Concerns About Immigration. Here Are the Facts." *Global News*, February
4, 2019. https://globalnews.ca/news/4794797/canada-negative-immigration-
economy-ipsos/.

Wallace, Sarah Isabel. 2017. *Not Fit to Stay: Public Health Panics and South
Asian Exclusion*. Vancouver: University of British Columbia Press.

Yeates, Neil. 2018. *Report of the Independent Review of the Immigration and
Refugee Board: A Systems Management Approach to Asylum*. April 10, 2018.
Ottawa: IRB Review Secretariat. https://www.canada.ca/content/dam/ircc/
migration/ircc/english/pdf/pub/irb-report-en.pdf.

York, Geoffrey. 2018. "Number of Asylum Seekers More than Doubles in Canada
in 2017: United Nations." *Globe and Mail*, June 20, 2018.

part one

COMING TO CANADA

Once a Refugee, Always a Refugee

GEORGE MELNYK

I was three years and four months old when I arrived in Halifax aboard the USAT *General C. C. Ballou,* a repurposed American troop ship that was bringing the "huddled masses" of post–World War II Europe to North America. It was December 1949. Sixty-seven years later to the month, I stood with a group of friends in the Calgary International Airport as we welcomed our privately sponsored Syrian refugee family to Canada. It seemed fitting for one refugee to welcome another refugee family to Canada in the same month they had arrived many years previously. It is such serendipitous moments that make this a story about linkages, those curious and often unseen or subconscious connections that ground refugees as they embrace their Canadian identity. It is also the story of anyone who has been forced to seek refuge in another country and then had to situate themselves in an unfamiliar place, culture, and language. That story began long ago.

Canada began offering a home to refugees when it was still a British colony. The American War of Independence (1776–83) generated British North America's first major influx of refugees, who consisted of British soldiers and United Empire Loyalists fleeing the newly created United States of America. The Loyalists journeyed to what was then called British North America mainly on ships from New York, just as I came by ship from Hamburg 170 years later. Yet, while these Loyalists were given "refuge" from the newly founded United States, they were also very useful to Great Britain, which needed to solidify its foothold in North America after having just lost a major portion of it in the war. The arrival of some forty thousand English-speaking newcomers also added significantly to the population of what had, until the end of the Seven Years' War (1755–63), been New France.

This influx of refugees needs to be juxtaposed with less positive moments in Canadian history. In 1758, during the Seven Years' War, the British captured the Fortress of Louisbourg, in what is now Nova Scotia, and began deporting French settlers to New Orleans, then still under French authority. It was, for all practical purposes, ethnic cleansing. Colonial Canada also provided a home to African American slaves who journeyed along the famed Underground Railroad in search of freedom. Travel along the railroad reached its zenith during the 1850s and 1860s, but fugitive slaves had begun arriving after the passage, in 1793, of the Act to Limit Slavery in Upper Canada. Although the act did not outlaw slavery, it prohibited the introduction of any new slaves, thereby ensuring that, once in Upper Canada, fugitive slaves would be free. Yet these freedom seekers were not the first ex-slaves to arrive in the Canadian colonies. They were preceded by the Black Loyalists—slaves who had fought on the side of the British during the American Revolution and were subsequently rewarded with emancipation and then resettled elsewhere, principally in Nova Scotia. While this may seem like a positive turn of events, we should remember that Britain did not abolish slavery within the empire until 1833. This meant that slaves who accompanied white Loyalists who had migrated to Canada were not automatically freed, a situation that understandably produced tensions. Moreover, even if slaves who made it to Canada were considered free, they were rarely equal: they faced discrimination because of the colour of their skin. In the century following Confederation, the image of Canada as a welcoming country would continue to be undermined by deportations, racially inspired immigration policies, and a selective openness with regard to refugees.

Unbeknownst to me as a toddler, I was part of that selective bias. After World War II, Canada was looking for inexpensive labour and while it painted its acceptance of European refugees as an act of humanitarianism, the decision was founded more on economics than anything else. As a white European family, we fit the profile the country wanted at the time. We were officially "displaced persons," but our displacement was to Canada's advantage as it accepted thousands of young men and women with the potential of contributing many years of useful employment to capitalists (manufacturing was then a cornerstone of the economy) and income taxes to the state. Canada needed strong bodies in the twentieth century as much as it needed them in the eighteenth. My father, whose origins were lower middle class, became a blue-collar factory worker for the rest of his life, while I embraced the promise of advancement that education offered.

Canada as a British colony preferred English-speaking migrants who felt bound to the mother country. But that was not always possible, especially as the United States became a nineteenth-century beacon to Europeans of all nationalities, thus allowing it to expand its population rapidly. An urgency developed in Canada to attract any white settlers that it could to offset the immigration juggernaut on its border. When British-occupied Ireland experienced a dreadful famine in the mid-nineteenth century, many Irish fled to Canada for relief and were accepted. And then in the 1890s, after the building of the trans-continental Canadian Pacific Railroad, the federal government advertised widely in Eastern Europe for settlers to occupy land on the Prairies that had been "surrendered" during the making of the Treaties. Hundreds of thousands eventually came. None of these new immigrants and refugees were of Anglo-Saxon origin, but they were taken in because of racially biased policies and acts that made immigration from other parts of the world, like China, difficult. If Canada wanted to populate/colonize the land that it had bought from the Hudson's Bay Company and had subsequently taken over by treaty from Indigenous peoples with European settlers, it had to look beyond the Anglo world. Fifty years before I arrived in Winnipeg, the so-called "Men in Sheepskin Coats" who were of my own ethnic group—Ukrainian—came West as settlers. That generation was mythologized for future arrivals like me. They were the forbears I knew nothing about. However, while Eastern Europeans were courted reluctantly, there was a racial line that the government would not cross. The thousands of Chinese labourers who had come to Western Canada to build the trans-continental railroad in the 1880s were asked to go home when the work was done; if they stayed they were prohibited by law from owning land and had to pay a punitive head tax aimed at discouraging Asian immigrants who wanted to bring their wives and families to Canada.

While I was ethnically connected to a much earlier migration, I was also ideologically connected to an earlier refugee story from the same region. The Doukhobors (Spirit-Wrestlers) were Russian religious pacifists who had been persecuted for their refusal to do military service under the Tsars. The famous novelist, Count Leo Tolstoy, sponsored many Doukhobors to make it possible for them to come to Canada in 1899 as a sanctuary from oppression. Here, they were exempted from military service and settled first in Saskatchewan as part of the colonization of the west, and later in British Columbia. My interest in the Doukhobors began in the 1980s when I was writing about cooperative and communal living in my book, *The Search for Community* (1984). It continued well into the twenty-first century, when I was active in the Consortium for Peace Studies at the University of Calgary because their story was part of the pacifist universe.

To compensate for its earlier generosity, the Canadian government passed an amendment to the Immigration Act in 1919 that effectively barred Doukhobors from entering Canada, along with such unlikely bedfellows as Mennonites and Communists because of their "peculiar customs, habits, modes of life and methods of holding property." Fortunately, less than a decade later the Mennonite Central Committee that had been formed in the United States to help their brethren in the Soviet Union, and which had a branch in Canada, was able to convince the Canadian government to lift this restriction because Mennonites were a persecuted religious and ethnic (German) minority in Communist Russia. Many of these pacifist Mennonites made it to Western Canadian. A few of them came to play important roles in my life, including a neighbourhood friend from my teen days in Winnipeg. Later, I met the famed Western Canadian novelist, Rudy Wiebe, in Edmonton and he became a big support in my early literary efforts as a magazine and book publisher and editor. Rudy had gone to a Mennonite school not far from where I lived in East Kildonan, Winnipeg.

This sometimes open- and sometimes closed-door approach to refugees is most evident in the racist criteria of the Immigration Act of 1910, which excluded Asians. In the case of African Americans, Canada played a Dr. Jekyll and Mr. Hyde role. It allowed thousands of former African American slaves who crossed on the Underground Railroad to settle in Nova Scotia, but a 1911 Order-in-Council tried to prevent African Americans from settling in Canada. The racist attitudes of the day reflected in official policy took a long time to overcome. We are still struggling to overcome many of the racist attitudes that are reflected in official policy of that time.

I remember a scene from my early childhood in Winnipeg in the 1950s. Our street was named Pacific Ave, and the population that lived in the neighbourhood was diverse, though we didn't use the term. One of the families was Japanese. I remember how the older Japanese boys would take on a phalanx of us younger immigrant kids in a mass snowball fight. Only much later as an adult did I learn that our Japanese neighbours had experienced deportation from their homes on the Pacific Ocean to internment camps deep in Canada during World War Two. These deportations and internments eventually garnered government apologies.

The threads that a refugee creates between distant histories, diverse ethnic groups, and the impact of their stories on his or her own life are necessary because they are the tendrils that nurture a sense of belonging. Without them there would a constant undercurrent of dislocation and alienation. Those who went before; those who suffered in a similar vein; and those who mirror one's own identity serve as the psychological foundations of belonging and identification. In my case a birth identity as a stateless person has remained with me, creating a psychological need to identify with all refugees, whatever their nationality or wherever their home. You might say that once a refugee, always a refugee.[1] I constantly cross paths with others of similar background.

For example, I was living in Toronto as a graduate student when Canada began an airlift of Ismaili Muslims from Uganda because they had been given an impossibly short notice to leave the country. Welcoming these Asian-origin Muslims was a departure from the Canada's earlier emphasis on allowing European refugees into the country. In 1967, a new Immigration Act officially ended racial discrimination by instituting a points system that applied equally to everyone, though the new system favoured certain classes and levels of education. The Ismailis were the first major group to benefit from the new approach. Many years later I also benefited from the Ismaili migration, when my closest colleague at the University of Calgary happened to be an Ismaili whose family had come from Tanzania in the mid-1970s. Although not officially a United Nations Convention refugee, my colleague came to Canada because of the economic pressures being put on this ethnic and religious group. When my colleague was an undergraduate in the 1980s, he was active in establishing the World University Service of Canada on campus that helped sponsor an Ethiopian refugee.

---

1 My mother wrote a poem many years ago titled "Eternal Refugee: Poem for Today."

In 1969, Canada finally signed the UN Convention Relating to the Status of Refugees, some eighteen years after it had been first adopted by the UN's General Assembly. In 1976, it passed a new Immigration Act, which recognized that Canada needed to make provision for the resettlement of refugees. One of the first beneficiaries of this policy were the Vietnamese boat people, some of whom were among the first refugees I helped.

One of the provisions of the new act was the establishment of options for the private sponsorship of refugees. These eventually included a category termed a Group of Five that enabled five or more individuals to collaborate in sponsoring a refugee. While we were living in Edmonton, my wife, who taught ESL to newcomers, and I worked with some friends of ours to use the Group of Five category to sponsor a young Vietnamese named Kiet for one year. Then we set up a non-profit group called Community Aid to Refugees Today (CART), which worked with churches and other private sponsorship groups that needed help dealing with refugees who did not speak English or were alone, were separated from their families, and whose culture was very different from that of their sponsors. We even got a bit of funding from the federal government to assist us in our efforts.

The provision for private sponsorship of refugees has been one of the great success stories of Canadian refugee resettlement. Over a quarter of a million refugees have come to Canada through this program, which is unique to Canada. Often privately sponsored refugees have done better in terms of resettlement than government-sponsored refugees have because of a voluntary hands-on involvement. The personal touch seems to work because it keeps the private sponsors directly connected to the issues that their refugees face daily—from accessing services to education to accommodation.

The exodus of the boat people was dangerous, costly in terms of refugee lives, and problematic because of long stays in camps in neighbouring countries. This desperate situation spurred Canadian church groups, led by the Mennonite Central Committee, to convince the federal government to establish a master agreement protocol that allowed an officially sanctioned body like the Anglican Church of Canada to serve as an umbrella for numerous private sponsorship groups. Individuals make donations to the Church for the charitable purpose of sponsoring refugees. The individuals get a tax receipt for their donation. They also work with their refugee family, while the Church supervises the Group of Five and is responsible for the family's well-being in case something goes amiss. The master agreement is a form of insurance that the refugee will be looked after properly because it involves a larger entity than just a group of five people. Having these master agreements has advanced private sponsorship and made it a viable and popular option for Canadians.

I have continued my work in this area thanks to the Group of Five category. The civil war in Syria (ongoing since 2013) has created millions of refugees, living either in camps in Jordan and Turkey or on the street in Lebanon. With the help of Lebanese friend, a group of us identified a UN certified Syrian refugee family living in Lebanon that we wanted to sponsor. So we created a new Group of Five called "Calgarians Give Back" that sponsored this family. They arrived in December 2017. At the same time, we learned of a couple from Serbia who were gay activists. They had suffered discrimination, persecution, and assault before coming to Canada on tourist visas. Using contacts in our Group of Five plus other friends, we raised $5,000 to pay their legal fees in applying for refugee status within the country. Fortunately, they were successful in their refugee claim. You can read their story in this book in the chapter titled "From LGBTQ+ Activist to Refugee."

In reflecting on my early status as a refugee and how it has affected my psyche, I now see that this particular identity has oriented me in certain directions and relationships that may not have occurred if I had been a non-refugee. In particular, I am referring to the large number of male Jewish friends I have had throughout my adult life and the near total lack of close Anglo-Canadian male friends. I have often wondered why this was the case because I am not Jewish myself. Having grown up in Winnipeg's North End, an ethnic ghetto with a large Jewish and Ukrainian population, I remain unsure of myself in an Anglo-Canadian social setting.

But there is more to this than simple ethnicity. Here, too, there is refugee resonance. One of my best friends and colleagues of the 1970s in Edmonton was the son of Holocaust survivors who settled in Canada after World War II. They and my friend, like my parents and I, came in the same wave of post–war migration. We were all refugees. I am sure it mattered in subconscious ways, and perhaps we connected on a personal level through these shared identities. Also, in the 1970s another friend whom I have known now for forty years was part of the wave of American war resisters who fled to Canada either to avoid the draft or because of their ideological opposition to the Vietnam War. Coming to a new land is something I understand and that I share with him.

This reference to friendships illustrates just one of the mysterious ways in which the refugee identity can manifest itself over time. I never would have imagined that my most satisfying friendships would entail men with a refugee background like mine. But it makes sense. We have a camaraderie first forged by historical circumstance and its narrative of displacement and persecution, and then cemented by a similar generational experience in a particular region of the country. So, when one of these friends and I sat in a Calgary café not so long ago, it was not surprising that we spent some of that time comparing our baby photos taken in post–World War Two Germany. As newborns we had no idea that we were refugees or what it meant to be one. Now we know.

The Best Place on Earth

VICTOR PORTER

My name is Victor Porter; I am sixty-three years old and live with my wife and children in Vancouver. I arrived in Canada as a government-sponsored refugee in April 1984. I was born and raised in Buenos Aires, Argentina, a grandchild of migrant Jews who left Poland and Ukraine in the earlier 1900s. From my earliest memories, the principles of justice and fairness were ingrained in me; I attended a state-run school in the morning and a liberal non-religious Jewish school in the afternoon. I have a very vivid memory of the moment in a class when we were studying the prophets. The teacher described the rage and wrath of God against those oppressing the people. That was the beginning of my understanding and my desire to become an *ish tzadik*, a just person.

Around the same time, when I was about nine years old, I began to understand more about my family history and started to piece together the family puzzle: my grandfather Jacob migrated to Argentina in the midst of the First World War to escape being drafted into the Polish Army. As soon as he could, he brought over my grandmother Ester and they settled in a working-class and immigrant neighbourhood in Buenos Aires called La Boca. He worked as an upholsterer in the Ford factory, and my grandmother started to sell work clothing to his co-workers. Eventually they opened a clothing store in the neighbourhood.

After the end of the Second World War, my grandparents devoted their time and money to reconnect with the very few relatives that had survived the Holocaust, and to bring them to Argentina. They were able to locate seven nieces and nephews and their spouses. They brought them to Argentina and supported them as they started afresh in a new country. All of them had been through a taxing journey, and had experienced tremendous losses, incarceration, trauma, and carried the added burden of being survivors when others were lost forever.

My cousins and I were curious children and wanted to know everything. At family events we would corner our uncles, Abraham and Shimon, and beg them to show us their concentration camp numbers tattooed on their arms and to tell us some stories. Shimon was reluctant, but he did. He had been a partisan and fought with the French resistance. Abraham barely shared anything. He had grey eyes and a very sad gaze. I now realize that whenever we forced him to talk about his experiences he was transported to another dimension, to a grey and ashen place.

My extended family and the familiar place of my Jewish afternoon school were my immediate reality. Then there was the outside real world, my state-run elementary school in which I was a minority among minorities. Most teachers were good, some excellent, but there were others who embodied the fascism ingrained in a significant portion of the Argentinian society. Take for instance our music teacher. I remember being in Grade 5 or 6 and having to march on the same spot on the bleachers while we sang the Federal Police anthem. The teacher seemed to hit the keys on the piano with inexplicable anger. Was this a music class? The country suffered successive dictatorships, with every new general trying to be more ruthless than his deposed predecessor. Their only interest in ruling the country was to protect the privilege of a few and to fight Communism.

One afternoon when I was ten, while I was having a glass of chocolate milk and crackers and watching the news after Jewish school, I learned about the capture and execution of Che Guevara. I still remember how that afternoon changed my life. The man who walked what he talked about was gone, only to return as an inspiration to me and countless more worldwide. By the time I was sixteen, I was a young political activist working with other students and neighbours on many issues related to poverty, supporting workers on strike, organizing impoverished tenants etc. Early in 1976, a new military junta established a dictatorship and started a plan of state-sponsored terror.

I clearly remember their chilling discourse: "First we will kill the enemies of the fatherland, then the subversive terrorists, then their supporters, then their families and friends, then the undecided." They did exactly that, or at least tried hard to. In the end, thirty thousand people disappeared. Only a small percentage of the bodies of those who disappeared were ever found. The alleged "enemies of the fatherland" were either killed "in combat" or "attempting to escape." Many more were incarcerated, including me.

After the junta came into power I, who was then eighteen, left Argentina only to return two years later, in 1978. For almost a year I distributed printed bulletins from the resistance, spray-painted anti-dictatorship graffiti, left leaflets in public places, markets, parks, and other activities like this. I also used television signals to broadcast messages from the resistance in areas of ten square urban blocks—this was prior to cable television. We were able to hijack the over-the-air TV transmission waves, blur the image, and replace the soundtrack with our broadcasted message. We usually timed our broadcasts to coincide with the local family dinner time between 8:30 and 9:00 p.m. This was also the time when the most popular TV shows aired. Barking dogs was one way for us to measure the success of our transmission: If the interference was successful, people started to scream, and dogs started to bark. All these efforts did not produce any tangible result other than to keep people's spirits up. The few activists left were disconnected and isolated. I was eventually arrested but the government did not acknowledge my detention for a week. I had "disappeared."

Torture, or "enhanced interrogation techniques" as some people have called it more recently, was a blanket approach applied to everyone from drunks to subversives. I, like everyone I later met in prison, was subjected to this treatment. Argentina abolished slavery and torture in 1813; however, its use was widespread. Electric cattle prods turned out to be excellent instruments to extract confessions and interrogate stubborn suspects. I was beaten badly and received successive applications of electricity, with armpits, gums, genitals, and nostrils being the favourite targets. Then there were the simulated executions. My hope throughout the torture sessions was to die soon, as soon as possible.

I consider myself lucky, very lucky, because at the time of my arrest I was very fit and was able to endure more and provide confusing answers. No person was subsequently arrested because of me, and this fact continues to give me peace of mind. I do not know what would have happened if the torture sessions had lasted half a minute more. I do not need to know, and I am grateful for this.

My family learned of my arrest/kidnapping through calls from witnesses. They immediately contacted my relatives in the United States of America and Mexico, and they in turn started to spread the word. I had lived for two years in Mexico and had made lots of friends while attending the Universidad Autónoma Metropolitana in Xochimilco. Upon learning of my detention, my Mexican friends organized a campaign to demand that the Argentinian dictatorship acknowledge my detention. The campaign included a march in front of the Argentinian embassy in Mexico City and the release of an Urgent Action bulletin by the Mexican branch of Amnesty International. I owe them my life. Because of these actions, the way I was treated changed. I was asked if I had "important" friends or family overseas. I answered: "Yes, very important" and played up the notability of imaginary friends and relatives.

A few days later I was recognized as a detainee and transferred from my secret place of detention to a police station, where I sat in a cell for a couple of days. At that point I realized that no matter what hardships awaited me in jail, I would survive. I also noticed how bad I smelled after a week in the inquisition place. It was a smell I had never produced before, and I have been very dirty in my life through camping excursions, sports, and so on. But no, this was different. It was a uniquely acrid and penetrating smell. Perhaps it was the smell of fear and primal survival, the chemistry and physiology of a body and a soul in turmoil. I was sleep deprived and had been without any food or water. The tortured are denied water because the electricity stored in a tortured body can be fatal when it is combined with water.

Eventually I was transferred to a regular prison where other political prisoners were held. The one I was held in was a 24-storey building with no windows, which meant the kept the fluorescent light on 24 hours a day. This jail was built with the purpose of housing regular detainees for a few days at a time in between court appearances, not as a permanent place of detention. However, the dictatorship recognized that this place was the perfect location to undermine our mental and physical health. I spent close to two years in that building. In addition to having the light on 24 hours a day, each cell consisted of three brick walls and a fourth one made of bars, identical to the kind of cage one would keep a monkey or a tiger in.

Our daily regime was called "Régimen de máxima peligrosidad," which means "Regime of maximum danger," and we the political prisoners were labelled as DT or DTS, which respectively stands for "terrorist delinquent" and "subversive terrorist delinquent." In addition, we were often raided by the *requisa*, a special unit within the guards. Their raids would coincide with political events taking place outside. The *requisa* would come to our floor armed with helmets and batons and Dobermann dogs. They would pull us from our cells, ransack our meagre possessions, destroy our writings, and then beat and humiliate everyone. We had to undress and expose ourselves in case we had a hidden weapon or a master plan for our escape or for defeating the dictatorship. They left as suddenly as they came, like a tornado leaving our lives to be picked piece by piece from the floor.

Sometime in 1981 I was transferred with others to another prison outside Buenos Aires, which was an older complex, with windows in the cells, and we were able to go to an outdoor patio a couple of hours a day. When we arrived, after almost two years with no direct natural light, even the guards at this prison were shocked by the colour of our skins, which had the appearance of a pale yellow parchment. "Where are you coming from?" they asked. "You look like ghosts!" Having a window was a big change for me, because I could look at the sky, the empty yard, barbed wire, the sun, the clouds and the rain. The days were slow and tedious and the regime continued to be abusive and humiliating—an attack on a fellow prisoner by officers and guards, mysterious landings of military helicopters in the field nearby and the possibility of being taken away again from prison for further interrogation. The only certainty was uncertainty. Yet we lived with that uncertainty day after day, trying to keep each other engaged with life, with ideas, with hope. We told stories, shared our knowledge, talked about everything we remembered, and read as many books as the censorious librarian allowed in.

One morning I had an epiphany. It was raining, the day was grey and everything looked like in a black and white movie. I was sitting by the window, drinking maté, our national tea. Everything was quiet, with only the noise of falling raindrops breaking complete silence. I could see the drops suspended on the barbed wire. I was mesmerized by the fact that the raindrops lasted so long hanging on the wire. I knew that they would inevitably fall. I was taken by the beauty of such a sad picture, and something became crystal clear to me: I was in the place a person like me should be in that moment in history—an imprisoned political prisoner. If I were not one, there were only three other options for me—living underground, being disappeared, or dead. I realized that despite the daily rigours of life in prison, the hunger and the anger, I could be here for as long as the dictatorship lasted and I would be just fine.

My grandfather Jacob had died many years before I was arrested, and yet he visited me in prison. I still have vivid memories of those dreams in which he visited me in my cell. He came and sat on the cement bench and we had lengthy conversations. In one dream I asked him, "How come they let you in?" and he responded: "I can go anywhere I want." When I think about my time in prison and what helped me endure, survive, and emerge from the experience more or less in one piece, I have to credit the unconditional love and care I got from my grandfather as a child, and of course his regular nocturnal visits. He was an important part of my being reconciled with my fate.

Another exceptional thing happened to me while in prison during Easter week in 1982. The regime allowed contact visits. Ordinarily we could only see our visitors through glass and communicate with them through a sort of hose or metal tube, but during this time we could see and embrace our visitors. Those of us receiving a visitor were taken to a large room. In that room I ran into Pedro, a friend who was held in another wing. I have not seen him for many months and was happy to have a few minutes with him. Then the visitors entered the room. My mother appeared with a young woman. I kissed my mother and was introduced to this young woman. "This is Maria Inés, Pedro's younger sister." I kissed the girl on the cheek as is customary in Argentina, and she carried on visiting with her brother. But for me, the world stopped, everything faded and went out of focus. I was semi-paralyzed in her presence. It felt like a silent thunderbolt had cut through me, had washed everything away, and for weeks I was in heaven and in hell at the same time, unable and unwilling to shake the impact of her presence.

On March 30, 1982, the Argentinian people mobilized and organized the first massive demonstration against the dictatorship. The police started to move on the demonstrators. In response, office employees from the buildings surrounding the demonstration started to throw everything they could get their hands on—glass ashtrays weighing two pounds were the projectile of choice—and many Army and police vehicles were damaged. The people had enough and, most crucially, acted in spite of their fear and the reign of terror they were subjected to.

Perhaps as a response, the junta launched an invasion of the Islas Malvinas (Falkland Islands) and declared war on England. There were a few weeks of patriotic euphoria that lasted only until the time it took for the British navy to cross the Atlantic and defeat our malnourished, trembling, and inexperienced eighteen-year-old draftees. Argentina lost the war, and that was the beginning of the end for the dictatorship. Shortly after the end of the war, the dictatorship allowed the International Committee of the Red Cross to visit the prisons where political prisoners were held to inspect and document the conditions. A few days later delegations from the Vatican, France, Holland, Denmark, and Canada were also allowed to visit the prisons and talk to the prisoners. As they heard our stories, and viewed the conditions in which we lived, their message was consistently the same. The foreign delegates said, "We are unable to get you out of prison, but as soon as you are out, we will get you out of the country."

I was released from prison around Christmas 1982, and I was picked up by my family. Also, a couple of other released prisoners came to my home to organize their return to other provinces where they had come from. The release was announced that very morning, and by the early evening we were at my house. Relatives kept arriving. It was a big day for everyone, as they all felt that they were recovering a part of them that had been taken away. My uncle Abraham, a Holocaust survivor, embraced me and said, "Now I have someone who understands me." And then he started to cry. To this day I believe that if my almost four years of being jailed as a political prisoner made my uncle Abraham feel understood by someone, then every minute of this journey was worth it. I came out winning. We came out winning.

At the same time, I regret the amount of pain and suffering that my detention caused to my parents and sister. My father, like many other fathers, was not able to come to terms with my being detained. He got extremely sick with a bone infection and endured a number of operations. My mother, and most of the other mothers I heard of, shouldered the agony of their sons and daughters being in prison or disappeared. They became the spine of Argentina's moral and social consciousness and are still in their late eighties and nineties the bastion of social justice. Following Canadian consular advice, I left Argentina after my release, and got my visa in another country. I landed in Vancouver in the spring of 1984 as a government of Canada sponsored refugee. Like many other newly arrived refugees, I struggled to learn English, to understand the country, and to find and make my way. I worked as a dishwasher, delivered newspapers, became a cook, a beekeeper, a production manager in the first tofu wiener factory in the country, a theatre practitioner, an advocate for immigrants and refugees, a coordinator for the British

Columbia government's response to human trafficking, a popular educator consultant, and most recently, an employee of the labour movement. I can still smell injustice from a distance and continue to work to do away with it.

Every morning, I wake up and from my bed I look at the trees lining my street. Next to me, Maria Inés is still asleep (yes, the girl who struck me like a thunderbolt arrived in Canada in 1987 to join me). We raised four children, who are more courageous, hard-working, compassionate, intelligent, and grounded than I ever will be. Every morning I know that I am in the best place on earth, and I am grateful for everything.

From Scars to Stars

FLORA TERAH

I came from Kenya, an African country where tea and coffee are grown. While tea and coffee are the main exports, Kenya's natural resources include limestone, gypsum, soda ash, diatomite, gemstones, fluorspar and even zinc. The expansive wildlife reserves and the white sand beaches of the coast bring out the country's beauty. It is also a land of women known for their resilience and inner strength.

My story begins here: "I cannot trust anyone; my girls and I were raped in that refugee camp and this one [pointing to a ten-year-old malnourished girl] is almost giving birth." These are not my words. They were told to me many years ago when I worked with vulnerable women in Kenya. Every day when I went to work, I knew that I would hear a story that would break my heart. Was I dressing the wound without treating it? Yes, I was. I was moving sand with a teaspoon.

It wasn't just this kind of violence that I encountered every day, it was also the poverty that Kenyan women suffered. There are many stories to tell, but how about I just write about the mother of four who had her children play all day as a pot of water boiled in her traditional African kitchen while she hoped that they would get tired and sleep because she had nothing to give them? Poverty in Kenya benefits the corrupt leaders who use it to profit from the business of importing maize and rice from Brazil. Poverty is a tool of the wealthy.

The government had misplaced priorities and we women had to step in to address economic marginalization and outdated cultural practices that mainly targeted women and girls. If Kenya were to have real change, we had to sponsor a bill that was favourable to women and we had to address affirmative action by bringing women to Parliament. This is how I found myself running for office as a member of Parliament. Having worked for close to nineteen years as a social worker, I had enough support so that there was no way the incumbent could have beaten me at the ballot. The opinion polls showed that I was likely to get elected. Those who were opposed to my candidature organized and arranged for me to be attacked by a gang of three men near my home. The attackers repeatedly warned me against running for the parliamentary seat. I was hospitalized for weeks by the assault and so was unable to canvass properly. I lost, but worse was to come because I had clearly stated that not even torture would stop me. As a result, my only child was brutally murdered. My case was highlighted in an Amnesty International report on the state of the world's human rights that was released on May 28, 2008. I had to leave the country for safety.

Even after my child's murder, I wanted to continue working and speaking out for the unheard voices: "How was it possible to speak from a country that knows so much privilege?" I asked myself as I flew into Toronto. I was aware that my education and experience might not necessarily carry the same level of importance as it did back home. I wasn't an economic migrant in search of greener pastures, so I thought my time in Canada would be temporary. Once the situation normalized, I would head back home to serve my people. That was never to be. I am now proudly Canadian.

Even though the English language was not a barrier, I knew that cultural differences meant we process messages differently. Even so, the weather, culture, and interaction were a bit of a scare to me. It took about two weeks to settle after I arrived in December. Even though I was enjoying people's concern for my welfare, my thoughts were fixed on Kenya, and grief was chewing at me. None of my hosts noticed that underneath my smile there was grief, worry, and pain. The story of the refugee woman back in Kenya, whose child was raped and heavily pregnant kept coming to mind as I watched Canadian friends toast my first Christmas in Ottawa. Thoughts continued to race through my head: "Soon I will have to go look for my own apartment and be on my own. What dangers will I face? Am I going to be as vulnerable as those women in my country I left back home? What opportunities do I have to continue fighting to redeem my son's spirit?" Nobody brought up the post-traumatic stress disorder, grief and depression that come with forceful relocation. There were simply some discussions to help one integrate into the Canadian society. So I continued with my cosmetic happiness, which went on for almost four years. There were missed opportunities and lost friends along the way because of my trauma. I even thought of ending my life. I assumed that people would see my pain when I told my story. There were university, school, and church talks where I told my story. I shared platforms with world-renowned leaders and won the hearts of many but afterwards went back home a very broken woman.

As I write this chapter, I am travelling back down the valley of darkness. I pass by the very raw wounds of desperate single mothers, past women trapped in outdated cultural practices and girls escaping female genital cutting, and finally arrive at my very own loss of my only child. This is a very heavy price to pay for liberating the women. And yet I wouldn't have known freedom of speech and what walking without looking behind one's back was like if I hadn't taken the bold step to say, "For my own safety, I will leave."

Nevertheless, my life inside was torn apart. Fleeing Kenya had sucked a substantial amount of self-confidence and self-esteem out of me. I needed help. I had to integrate into society and find meaningful employment. I was given a contract by a well-known organization that worked in Africa. This made me more comfortable financially and allowed me to meet women who were willing to listen. After my contract ended, I went to Montréal to search for work and to volunteer in a community centre. I did not speak French. It was a mistake to move to Montréal. I was vulnerable and had this mental illness that needed professional help more than employment. I got a part-time job but was unable to help myself from within. I was trapped in my own world and no one could see this. I was literally living in a glass prison. I watched and listened to people's beautiful ideas and advice on where they wanted me to be, but the ME inside was hurting and in need of intensive care. When the psychological pain got worse, I tried easing it by cutting my wrists. I would go to work with bandages. Finally, I ended up with a serious panic attack and was hospitalized. This was the first time I had a mental health professional attend to me. After about a year in Montréal, I came to my senses and started preparing myself to relocate back to Toronto where there were familiar multicultural organizations and the benefit of being in an English-speaking province. I made this decision on my own, with the support of my friends and my medical professionals.

I had been in Canada almost three years and I swore to make it or break it. I made up my mind that I would give back to the country that had adopted me. I started volunteering at the YMCA to help newcomers to integrate into the Canadian society. Most of them spoke openly of their own struggles and finally accepted professional help. I was very happy about this because I had done the same thing. I knew I was helping fellow immigrants and refugees find themselves. I knew I was contributing in the spirit of my adopted country. I had come to realize that Canada is one big social experiment. It has blended people from all corners of the earth, from different cultures, different backgrounds, and different faiths into one family. That is the diversity that makes Canada unique. This even made me fall in love with the country. I began searching for the application forms for citizenship (the ones that I had sworn to my friends I would complete over my dead body)—I started looking for them as someone searching for oxygen. My wishes came to pass, and I became a Canadian citizen. I voted and I loved every bit of my constitutional rights. I sang "Oh Canada" loudly and proudly.

I had been speaking to students in high schools, universities, and other institutions around Canada from the time I arrived. I did not even understand the impact I was making on these communities. Year after year I started being nominated for, and receiving, awards. At some point I had a very candid discussion with my friend, Sue. She was driving me home one evening after dinner and I asked her to give me an honest opinion about the nature of these awards because I felt kind of flattered. I explained that what I had done in my motherland was much more than what I was doing in Canada and yet no one had even toasted that with a cup of tea in Kenya. Was my reception in Canada genuine?

Sue told me that Canadians were genuine. They are touched by everything that I said and have done. I had volunteered throughout the years I lived here and even the speaking engagements were part of the spirit of Canadian volunteerism. Many organizations had heard my cry for help and had started supporting grassroots organizations. This is when I understood that even though I was not physically serving my people as I had wanted, I was doing something indirectly. School children had started donating for things like boreholes. I remember a twelve-year-old named Noah who came to visit me with his grandmother to tell me that they had donated $1,000 for water in Kenya. Through my speaking engagements, I found my voice in Canada. I feel fulfilled when I speak from my heart. This is why my next goal is to run for political office.

I hope to work on the issues affecting immigrant women and children. For example, when the Trudeau government was contemplating removing references to FGM/C (female genital mutilation or cutting) as a harmful practice from the citizenship guide, I lobbied a couple of members of Parliament in Ottawa to speak out against this. Thankfully, they heard our voices and didn't do it. I felt that removing FGM/C would encourage immigrants who are already taking their children abroad for this outdated act. Based on the 2011 Canadian Census and UNICEF's statistics on the prevalence of FGM/C in the affected countries of Africa, there are probably tens of thousands of girls living in Canada who are potentially at risk.

I know women who say they would like to take their children back to Africa on a prolonged holiday when they come of age. People assume that the girls are being taken back to learn about their background and traditions. But what they do not know is that often these traditions involve the most harmful and outdated cultural practices that the newcomers have refused to unpack. The authorities will never know about it because the girls are taken through trauma and so much pain and fear that they will not report what happened to their teachers or friends. I have worked with these communities to end female genital circumcision, so I understand their coded language. Some of the women that I speak to are afraid to be sent back to Africa if they say anything in Canada. As one way of dealing with this issue I started a legacy dinner in memory of my late son. Through this dinner, I generate funds to continue working on violence against women.

I also founded an organization named the Wanawake Violence Prevention Team. I started training women in the Wellness Recovery Action Plan that had helped in my recovery. I did not have any finances to run the organization so I decided that I would embrace tiny victories and do much with little. I had been an educator on HIV/AIDS and I knew very well that discussion groups under a tree back in Africa worked and cost nothing. I decided to focus on violence against women and this is what I ran with. Many women have started speaking out and it is through this that they are getting back their voices. The more I continue advocating for change and addressing matters of violence against women, the more stories are coming out. This is a very crucial time for women's civic education and that of girls too. The hashtag #MeToo has encouraged women to speak out about sexual violence. While living in North America I have learned that it is easier to raise this issue and increase awareness because there is sex education in schools. In Africa, talking about sex and death is taboo. If I tried to speak about sex and violence in Africa, I would be told that I am influencing girls in a bad way and bringing Western values to young ones. However, girls everywhere are learning from social and electronic media that have become substitute parents to them.

The most fundamental issue of my relocation to Canada has been coming to terms with my mental illness, which was prolonged by my failure to seek medical help and by Canadians not knowing how to respond because of my cosmetic smiles and my confidence in moving on. The tradition of holding emotions in I inherited from my mother, who I never saw cry until the day my son's casket was being lowered in the grave. After my son's death and seeing her cry, I literally sat on her lap and wept uncontrollably. That was when I felt the real pain my mother was going through. After seeking professional help, I could not understand why I was still depressed even though I was taking medication. I later joined a variety of recovery programs that provided me with fundamental ways of dealing with my condition. This has made a tremendous difference to my mental health. I even started talking to my friends who had their loved ones living with mental illness. I have become a volunteer peer support specialist who works with those with a mental illness, and I passionately love what I do. I want to continue advocating for people living with mental illness and their families because I discovered that shutting in pain and wearing cosmetic smiles and exhibiting false confidence only destroys you in the end. We need to understand that the suitcases newcomers come with are not just physical ones. They have other pieces of baggage that no one sees. I had PTSD. Hugs, words of support, and comfort were not enough. I needed medical attention.

Finally, I want to say something about the role of Canadian organizations that work in Africa. While I have worked and volunteered with quite a few grassroots organizations, I find it hard to understand why they never use the immigrants and those that come from a particular region to monitor and evaluate their funded programs. Canadians without any background in Kenya are being sent to my motherland to evaluate and monitor programs. They need interpreters in order to do their work. Similarly, we would be much better off if African governments were held accountable by their development partners. Foreign governments should fund grassroots and other not-for-profits because the millions of dollars sent to governments end up in the hands of a few individuals.

Since I left the country of my birth, Kenyan women leaders have changed the dynamics of political engagement. More and more women are open to leading in all spheres. Thankfully, they operate under a new constitution with more openness to women's participation. Because of mentorship and a free sanitary towel program, teenage girls attend school all the time, which wasn't the case before. Change is not easy, and many people are afraid of it. However empowering women around the world is an idea whose time has come. It was my choice to relocate to Canada and I am glad Canada accepted me. Now I am rebuilding my entire life while remaining an advocate for women's rights.

Fleeing The Gambia

MATIDA DAFFEH

I came from The Gambia, a West African country of about two million people. I am a permanent resident in Canada now and have my eight-year-old son who joined me in 2018. Many beautiful people and organizations have stood by me and have helped me to integrate in Canada. I am a feminist and social justice activist, and an anti-female genital mutilation (FGM) advocate who is passionate about equality between women and men. I have worked with non-governmental and community-based organizations at both local and sub-regional levels, for the past twelve years of my life. My work is centred on women's human rights issues, including advocating for women's land rights, political representation and inclusion in community development initiatives, and the elimination of harmful traditional practices such as female genital mutilation and child marriages.

The last organization I worked with in Africa before coming to Canada was United Purpose (UP), formerly called Concern Universal. Concern Universal benefited from a four-year project funded by the United States Agency for International Development (USAID), which sought to promote sustainable development using a people-to-people approach. My main function in this project was to ensure gender mainstreaming, which included ensuring the full participation of women and youth at all levels of the project—from design and implementation to monitoring and evaluation. I also assessed capacity gaps and built the capacity of community-based organizations to help them understand the nature and consequences of gender-based violence. My work also centred on gender mainstreaming, gender-sensitive budgeting, and proposal development. In addition, I encouraged organizations to develop gender policies to avoid discriminatory practices. During this period, I lived in the conflict zone of Casamance in southern Senegal, but I would return often to The Gambia where we had some project partners. In addition to my work at UP, I was the chairperson of The Girls' Agenda (TGA), a community-based organization that I co-founded with some friends. TGA was born out of the desire to contribute to changing the cultural/traditional practices that negatively impact the lives of women and girls.

On February 3, 2016, an online newspaper, *What's On—Gambia*, reported that the party leader of the United Democratic Party, the main opposition party in The Gambia, had stepped down and selected one Matida Daffeh (me) as their flag-bearer for the presidential election that was few months away. The news went viral. While most young people supported the idea of a woman standing for the presidency, some people were against it, especially when that person was someone as young as me. Knowing the kind of political atmosphere in The Gambia, many people, including my friends and family, feared for my life.

I was facilitating a training session at our sub-regional office in Senegal when messages started pouring into my phone. Friends, acquaintances, former colleagues, former school- and classmates, and journalists were all trying to reach out to me. By habit, my phone was either on silent or vibrate mode, which helps me avoid being distracted unnecessarily. During a short break, I checked my phone and saw a few congratulatory messages. Most of the messages were from people trying to verify the news, or from journalists requesting interviews. I was too busy to respond. I switched off the phone again. Maybe I underestimated the seriousness and possible damage this could have on my life. A few minutes later, my project manager came in and told me to answer an official call from our head office in Banjul. I held my breath. This must be something serious, I thought. I had to convince my manager that what they saw on the news was not true. UP was once threatened with closure by the former Gambian president, so they tried as much as possible to protect their image.

I began to feel restless. I went back to the training, but then I spent that entire evening talking with some of my friends and family, most of whom provided me with emotional support, even though they were scared to the core. Many said that the long-time president, Yahya Jammeh, would come after me for sure, so I should run for my life. I responded that I hadn't committed any crime that should warrant running away. To further justify my point, I would sarcastically ask, "Is it a crime to express interest in politics?" After all, I was not even friends with *What's On—Gambia* on Facebook, so what on earth could make me their target? Could it be that they followed my activities without me knowing? Of course, I did promote social justice issues. I also promoted women's political representation and I shared posts relating to it. Once I shared a post in which I asked if The Gambia was ready to have a female president. In response to their hoax, I wrote on my Facebook wall that the news was false. I also granted interviews to a few local journalists in the country, during which I expressed my disappointment about the publication of such an unfounded story.

Two days later, the head of the opposition party also cleared the air through local newspapers. All of these actions did not satisfy Jammeh and his cronies. He used his secret agents as he always did. They pursued me and threatened my life. I was puzzled as to why I was targeted. Out of the many strong women in The Gambia, why was I singled out? Was it because of the work I did and the radical way with which I challenged things? I had spoken out against the practice of polygamy in 2015, and my comments were published by a local newspaper. After the publication appeared, some people, including some friends and comrades, called to caution me. Many people expressed their dissatisfaction with me as a daughter of a religious scholar who also practiced polygamy. Although many people, especially the younger generation of women, do not support the idea of polygamy, it is often not discussed because of its sensitive nature.

Human rights defenders and feminist activists were prone to arbitrary arrest and torture during Jammeh's dictatorship in The Gambia. I was not an exception. I started receiving threatening messages from unknown people. I was not affected deeply until someone wrote a letter to TGA, the grassroots organization where I served as chairperson. According to the letter, the police were investigating the presence of a government official at a training program on FGM and sexual violence against girls organized by TGA. Some TGA members were taken to the police station for questioning. I started fearing for my life, and my mother became even more scared.

My mother was in poor health and so I knew I could not possibly run and leave her and my then three-year-old child behind. I had to face the police.

On March 7, 2016, I met with both the National Intelligence Agency and personnel of the serious crime unit of the Gambian police. Prior to going to the meeting that morning, I woke my child up from bed, kissed and hugged him, and whispered to him that should he never get to see me again, I had committed no crime. I was just a victim of circumstance. This was perhaps the most traumatizing moment for me. I wept holding my child. During the interrogation, I was terrified, but I refused to show any sign of fear, for this might be used to their advantage. They asked if I had any affiliation with any political party, and whether or not I had any interest in becoming president. They wanted to know what type of activities I was engaged in, the organizations I worked with, and my primary responsibilities. They also asked whether or not I was married, and other questions in this vein. Most of the questions where personal and I guess this was a deliberate act to provoke me. Only once did they refer to the person they were supposedly interested in. The rest of the time it was all about me and my political aspirations. After hours of interrogation, they warned me not to leave the country without notice. The investigation had just begun, they said, and it would continue. I told them I had no intention of leaving the country. I had not committed any crime. I continued my work in both The Gambia and Senegal. I restricted my movements and stopped attending late-night events for security reasons. This was my life until August of the same year, when I had the opportunity to attend a Women's Human Rights Education Institute in Canada at the University of Toronto.

In September 2016, while in Canada, I got news that Dr. Isatou Touray, who was one of my feminist mentors and who had been instrumental in the fight against FGM and other traditional practices that violate the rights of girls and women in The Gambia, had expressed interest in contesting the coming presidential election. This made my case even more sensitive, so I filed for asylum. I wasn't sure what my fate would be, whether or not I would be granted asylum. I was worried about many things: I had left The Gambia two days after my child's fourth birthday and I was missing him badly. I also missed my mother, who was very worried about my safety and general well-being. I missed my work and my community. I had no idea how long it would take to reunite with my family, friends, and community. In a family of over twenty, I was the only one abroad other than a half-sister who lives in Spain with her husband and children.

I wondered if I would ever be welcomed in my new environment, or whether I would have any sense of belonging in my new environment. One thing I had always been told about Canada was that it is a tolerant and multicultural society, so that gave me hope. One organization that was instrumental in my asylum claim process was the Mennonite Coalition for Refugee Support (MCRS). They deal with refugee issues in the Kitchener and Waterloo area of Ontario. They made the application process bearable. They guided me through all the steps of the application process. I could not have imagined how to do this without such support. Further, MCRS linked me to Open Homes, a group of people who provide shelter for refugees in their homes. My experience with Open Homes was amazing. I stayed with an awesome couple, Cheryl Belch and David Clayworth, for about eleven months before I moved to Toronto to start my university program. They gave me support I never expected. They helped me through my integration process in Canada. They made their home a place I could call home.

I was afraid that my lawyer might not understand feminist issues. I began to be anxious even before meeting him. One of my friends connected me with the Barbra Schlifer Clinic. At the clinic, I received great support from the women I met. I shared my story with them, and we went through it together. The staff at Barbra Schlifer helped me get through my anxiety. They explained the court setup to me and advised that I get my evidence right. This was very helpful; at least I got someone to look at my case with a feminist lens. This was a relief. However, I was still worried about whether my male lawyer would understand my story. I needed a lawyer with a feminist perspective, yet I had limited control.

I had my first appointment with my lawyer, James Schmidt, in October 2016 and we were to meet at his office in downtown Kitchener. Although my case worker at MCRS told me many positive things about him, including his long experience of working on immigration issues, I remained skeptical. To my great surprise, James Schmidt made me as comfortable as I could be. He had worked with some Gambians before and had a sound knowledge of the country. I regained my confidence and was open to sharing my story without any feeling of guilt or being judged. We worked closely together and within three weeks, I was fully prepared for my hearing. I went to the hearing with him and Cheryl and everything went well.

A few months after the hearing, I got a call from my family that my mother was sick but that it was nothing to worry about. Within two days I got news of her demise. I got the news on the fateful morning of May 19, 2017. I struggled hard to convince myself that I was merely dreaming. It could not possibly be true that I had lost my mom while I was away. I thought of all the emotional trauma my mother endured because of me, and I began to tremble. I felt guilty and sad that I could not be there to mourn with the rest of the family. The stress of my persecution and of leaving the country must have been too much for her. After some fifteen minutes of deep thinking, I began to cry uncontrollably. I could not bear this alone. I needed someone to speak to, yet I wasn't sure if it was culturally okay to share my pain with Cheryl and David. I managed to reach out to Cheryl and to this day I am grateful that she provided me with a shoulder to lean on. I later contacted a Gambian friend who took me to stay with them for a couple of weeks. At this darkest moment in my life, I felt good to know that people you are not biologically related to could love and care so much.

I am grateful that I am able to pursue my dreams despite all the challenges. I am studying at the University of Toronto, majoring in women and gender studies and minoring in African studies, an area I have always been interested in. However, studying full-time while being a single parent is challenging; there are days that I feel overwhelmed, but am grateful for the support I receive from both the registrar's office and the Family Care office where I also serve as a student-parent mentor. My child has fully integrated at a school for the deaf and I am working on improving my ASL (American Sign Language).

I am now able to fully concentrate on school and pursue my dreams. I intend to continue my work as a social justice activist. As hard as it is, I am ready to take on this exhausting, risky, yet very fulfilling cause. While I am grateful for all the beautiful things this country has offered to me and my son, I also recognize that it is not a perfect country and that racial inequalities exist. My ultimate dream is to contribute to the dismantling of gender inequality, push back against colonial and patriarchal ideals such as sexism, ableism, Islamophobia, and heteronormativity. I believe that a just, better world is possible.

From LGBTQ+ Activist to Refugee

BOBAN STOJANOVIĆ

In the autumn of 1998, a friend of mine invited me to become part of her project. I was to create an educational play for children who lived in refugee camps all over Serbia. The play covered three stories about three topics: education, friendship, and personal hygiene. I thought it would be easy to do because I had some previous experience working on a refugee project. During the war that broke up Yugoslavia (1991–2001), I had helped at a camp for refugees not far from my hometown. The camp was crowded with people from Bosnia, Croatia, and Kosovo. Some were young, healthy, and seemingly ready to fight for life, while others seemed weak and exhausted. Thanks to all of them, I realized that becoming a refugee is not the end of life, but a rebirth. I accepted the invitation.

During rehearsals for this new Serbian project, we had to decide about props—just something simple, because we would be playing in a limited space. Everything had to fit into one trunk. Our first performance was in a big house located in a village in central Serbia. This villa belonged to the Serbian Royal Family, who ordinarily used it as a weekend home. But now it was filled with refugees from Bosnia and Croatia. When we approached the building, I saw women who were doing laundry by hand and men who were standing around smoking in the courtyard. They watched us carefully. The only sounds were those of children screaming, crying, and laughing. Theirs were the only human sounds in that environment.

The children were happy to have us there because somebody was doing something for them. Every place was the same: people without basic things, people full of fears and suspicions, and kids who wanted to be accepted. Clearly, acceptance is something that anyone who is marginalized struggles to find. Although I had sympathy, I could not identify with these refugees. I was living in my own country, with access to education and health care; I had my family and a cozy apartment. When I was not happy with what my grandmother decided to cook for dinner, I ordered pizza or some meat. I couldn't imagine becoming a refugee because I lived in a democratic country, although not a perfect one. But my experience with those refugee children made me aware of how life can take a turn for the worst. For me, a refugee seemed to be a person who doesn't have a choice. Then it was my turn to be a refugee.

The moment my partner and I decided to leave our country was the moment we became tired. On the way back from a meeting in August 2016, I was assaulted both verbally and physically. It happened in the middle of the day in the centre of Belgrade. But it was not the assault that was so disturbing (I had had to deal earlier with numerous incidents of one kind or another), but the reaction of the observers. I was quickly surrounded by about fifteen people who just watched without any reaction. Obviously, they viewed the assault as something that did not involve them. They were not under attack and had no interest in or sympathy for the victim. Maybe they were also afraid. Later, after another futile visit to a police station to report the assault, my partner and I decided to leave the country. Reporting the attack was futile because, like all the other incidents that we had reported earlier, it would never be solved. One of the worst of the previous attacks had come in 2013 when a neo-Nazi group called Combat 18 (18 was the symbol of Adolf Hitler's acronym and stood for the first and eighth letters of the alphabet [A and H]) smashed our windows and left a threatening note on our door.

As a visible gay activist, I had had enough. My country was not safe for me. I felt like a sick dog that had been kicked out of the house and left to wander. Our application for a tourist visa to come to Canada was approved very quickly. My partner, Adam, and I arrived two months later with four suitcases, a collection of perfumes and our beloved cat, Macy. It was the first day that the new international terminal at the Calgary airport was open, and we were on the first flight to go through the new customs and immigration area. We received an enthusiastic welcome, including the waiving of the $30 entrance fee for Macy. This country is promising, I thought to myself. Life here will be better. Learning about the new society is not easy at all.

The first time I came to Canada was by invitation. I was there as an International Grand Marshal during Pride Week in Montréal in August 2014. I found the LGBTQ+ community so connected. When I was introduced to someone, I received hugs and kisses. Going past the gay bars I got compliments. Getting such a comment in the middle of the street was strange to me because of the kind of animosity I had experienced on the streets of Belgrade. For me, that reflected freedom. Canada looked like heaven on earth.

We came to Canada again in 2016 with the intention of applying for refugee status after we arrived. We met people who helped us financially with hiring a lawyer to help us with our application. We got library cards and opened a bank account. We had a place to stay and we found people everywhere smiling and saying sorry and thank you. Strangers held a fundraising dinner for us, and we saw a United Church wrapped in rainbow flags. It all seemed so unreal, so different from our lives in Serbia. For the first time in my life I did not have the weight of political responsibility on my shoulders. I was physically here, but as a refugee claimant I was in limbo. Once our application was accepted and favourably adjudicated, which only took a few months, we began the task of integrating into Canadian society. As protected persons, we had the right to work while waiting for our permanent residence papers to arrive (a much longer process). My new life in Canada began with more questions than answers. Who am I now? What can I offer society? How will Canadians see me? All these questions revolved around the issue of identity because identity is the fundamental issue facing all refugees who have surrendered their past realities.

As my new life unfolded, I began rethinking my perception of refugees. My life became one of lost privileges, limited rights, dependence on elementary things, and the inability to make any plans. Also, uncertainty. However, there is one liberating moment in the decision to become a refugee—there is no tomorrow. From the moment when we decided to leave Serbia till the moment when the Immigration Board member announced his positive decision regarding our claim, we were in a strange way free. We no longer had passports. We didn't have any money to speak of. We didn't have a house. We didn't have anything to lose because we had given all of it up. We left our lives in the hands of the people who offered us help. We believed in the power of people more than ever. But we also learned to respect what the future would bring.

Besides the nerve-wracking experience of going through the refugee application process (our basis of claim was 23 pages long!) that so absorbed us, we also had time to reflect on our work and suffering in Serbia. Being LGBTQ+ activists in a corrupt society was not easy. Fear, blackmail, and insecurity are integral parts of a corrupt society, and anyone who is a rebel and insists on the truth and on their rights becomes an outsider. I learned very early in my life that every single person must fight for justice. My parents were members of labour unions in the companies they worked for and advocated for a better position for the workers. My grandfather was a dedicated Communist in a high-ranking position. He was one of those who believed in the Communist system and the idea that all people are equal. I could not become anything but an activist.

When I joined the peace, feminist, and LGBTQ+ movements in Serbia, there was very little activity regarding LGBTQ+ rights. For the next fifteen years after becoming involved, I fought for our rights. My activism took me from holding workshops in small towns for just a few people to speaking in front of almost half million people at Roma Pride. It took me from sleeping on the bus during a long journey home from a distant city to having my own driver as a Grand Marshal at Montréal Pride. But the struggle remained uphill, whether I was in a big or small venue. I remember vividly when someone spat in my face on the very day I was named one of the top five most prominent LGBTQ+ activists in the world.

My activism included discussions with politicians. Most politicians treat people as either tools or commodities to be exploited, so I always wanted to challenge their attitudes. From my feminist friends I accepted the idea that disobedience to the system is a vital factor in trying to change society. So when officials demanded that I wear a suit, I wore my favourite activist T-shirt. When others carried expensive leather notebooks at some VIP event, I carried my ordinary one covered with LGBTQ+ stickers. I never wanted to become part of the establishment just to be accepted. I believed that I should speak publicly about my life, repression, love, and all that I had experienced. I was a guest on political talk shows in Serbia, but also a participant in the local version of Big Brother. I gave a TED talk and wrote a book about my life, but I also spent nights answering questions from young

LGBTQ+ people who wanted to commit suicide. In a small, post-communist and post–war country, where many human values seem to have disappeared, my goal was to organize Pride. And I did.

With a group of dedicated people, we made changes that we could only dream about a few years earlier. Serbia Pride is more than a celebration of LGBTQ+ rights. After all the wars in the region where I lived, I found Pride to be a place to show our ability to love, to show our willingness to cross borders, to rise above nation and religion, to be above separation and hate, and to accept and learn from everyone who is different from us. But it was a hard job. In Calgary, we attended the LGBTQ+ group at Hillhurst United Church and became clients at the Centre for Newcomers in Calgary, and we got to celebrate Canada's 150th birthday on July 1, 2017. It was all so relaxed and wonderful compared to our life as activists in Serbia.

An important milestone in a refugee's life occurs when the refugee begins contributing to their new society. A refugee wants to give something back. As a political activist, I recognize the importance of sharing our story and our experience with others. I have given numerous speeches all over Alberta, and together with my partner I volunteer in many organizations in Calgary. Adam has decided to continue his education, which was abruptly cut off in Serbia because of discrimination against gays. But I chose to seek work so that we could survive economically. My first job in Canada, which I still have, was as a Settlement Practitioner at the Centre for Newcomers. The centre is supportive of LGBTQ+ newcomers and refugees. I am using all my knowledge and connections from my past as an activist and organizer to make Canadian society a better and more inclusive place. Like me, LGBTQ+ refugees from around the world who come to Canada need time to heal and to build trust in people and institutions. I am happy to help. And there is a lot of help that is needed.

When I started working at the Centre for Newcomers, I learned never to tell clients that they were completely safe. Canada is a society like any other society: unpleasant things happen here too. One of the unpleasant things is bureaucracy. The process of becoming part of Canadian society involves the completion of numerous application forms. Countless times, the same questions are asked, and the same answers are given. I am sure Canadians are unaware of the amount of paperwork that refugee claimants face. Moreover, after filling in the forms there is the endless waiting for the response. What is most unsettling is not being able to communicate with a human being in the government about one's application. The only available option is going online, and online the status is always "In process." In our case, I imagined that an envelope with our application was lying unopened on some desk in an office somewhere in Canada. Moreover, that it would stay there forever. I was upset and sad. The acceptance I felt on my first visit to Montréal did not exist in the government bureaucracy. Sometimes I even wondered whether I am welcome here. In the process of seeking asylum, the waiting and failure to know are the most difficult, even though my position at the Centre for Newcomers offers a privileged insight into the system. Honestly, sometimes I think the whole system, no matter how good, is inhumane.

Today when I can help other LGBTQ+ asylum seekers, I often ask them: Do you feel like this? They mostly say, with tears in their eyes: Yes. They ask how I know. I tell them: I was there. Perhaps my thoughts are utopian, but I believe that there should be people somewhere in the system who can be contacted in person. I know that being lonely is difficult. People need human support. Asylum seekers need to find someone who can provide a package of tissues when they face difficult times. No online application can replace a warm human word or understanding. While I was waiting for different decisions on various permits and changes in immigration status, I was confused and wondered if I was the only one who felt nervous. After a year of working with LGBTQ+ asylum seekers, I understood that I was not alone in that feeling. My partner and I were lucky enough to meet very supportive people. Although we do not have our families and our parents have died, we feel like we have "Canadian" parents. When someone finds themself in a position to leave their whole life behind and radically change their life by seeking asylum, they deserve to have someone answer their questions. An answer is not just an answer, it is the meaning of life.

I came to this country with hope for a better life, and that hope has been realized. While I am creating a new identity for myself that reflects my values, my beliefs, and my aspirations of equality and justice for everyone, I realize that a positive new identity is what I also wished for the refugee children that I worked with so long ago. Their road and my road to belonging now intersect. The look in their eyes has, in a way, become my look as well.

part two

CANADA RESPONDS

The Ugandan Asian Expulsion, 1972

A Personal Memoir

MICHAEL MOLLOY

I had always wanted a job that included international travel and was delighted when I heard in April 1968 that my application to join the foreign service of the new Department of Manpower and Immigration (M&I) had been accepted and that I was to report to M&I's national headquarters (NHQ) in Ottawa in June. We, that is, my wife Jo, our toddler Kathleen, and I, drove to Ottawa from Golden, British Columbia, in our Volkswagen Beetle. The training for our class of twenty-six new employees was extensive and included four weeks divided between two visa offices abroad, in my case Vienna and Belfast. I never got to Belfast because three days before my departure from Ottawa in August 1968, Soviet forces invaded Czechoslovakia to crush efforts by the Czechoslovakian government to introduce a more humane brand of Communism. Our Vienna office was flooded with applications from people who had managed to escape to Austria before the Soviets sealed the border. I was instructed to stay in Vienna and spent most of the next six weeks checking files and signing visas while more experienced officers interviewed the refugees. I then returned to Ottawa to complete my training and, with my wife, to complete formalities for the adoption of our new son, William.

Our family was then posted to Japan for a two-and-a-half-year assignment. The job consisted of shuttling between Tokyo and Seoul to interview people from Japan and Korea who wanted to immigrate to Canada. In family reunification cases, the purpose of the interviews was to verify family relationships. For independent immigrants, that is, those wishing to settle in Canada for economic reasons, the interviews were used to ensure that the individuals were qualified to come to Canada under the new "point system," which came into effect in in 1967 and applied to all those seeking to immigrate to Canada regardless of their origins.

We all enjoyed our time in Japan, but I was delighted after two-and-a-half years with the news of a new assignment in Beirut, Lebanon. We arrived in Beirut in November 1971, just in time for me, as the new guy in the embassy, to play Santa Claus at the embassy Christmas party. I had joined the foreign service to see the world, and you could see a lot of it from the Beirut immigration area office, which covered thirty-eight countries that stretched from Iran to Zambia. The four Beirut-based visa officers, who now included me, were always travelling.

In late January 1972 I made my first "area visit" to countries in East Africa and to one, Mauritius, in the Indian Ocean. When I showed my travel plan to the boss, Roger St. Vincent, he told me to include Kampala, Uganda, even though we had no immigration applications from that country. Roger explained that after the recent coup that had ousted the elected president Milton Obote and had installed General Idi Amin, he was worried that things might get worse for Uganda's small Asian community. I was to familiarize myself with the city and the airport, meet the leaders of the various Asian communities, and gather any information I could from the British and American missions there.

NEXT STOP, KAMPALA

As there were no direct flights from Beirut to East Africa at that time, the trip began with a flight to Athens to connect with an Olympic Airways flight to Kenya. I conducted two weeks' worth of interviews in Nairobi, then continued to Lusaka for three days, after which I flew to the beautiful island of Mauritius for another two weeks. Then it was back to Nairobi, where I had more interviews waiting. As directed, I spent four days in Kampala meeting everyone that I could. From them, I learned that the community leaders thought that they would be able to work with President Amin. Heading home, I stopped for three days' work in Addis Ababa, then transited through Cairo en route home to Beirut. The months that followed were spent doing routine immigrant interviews in Lebanon and going on a short working visit to Turkey.

By mid-June it was time for another marathon area visit to Africa, this time including a week-long stop in Dar es Salaam, Tanzania, where Asian businesses were being nationalized. Canada was destination of choice for those whose livelihood was being lost. In Kampala, things were no longer looking hopeful, and I spent a disturbing hour listening to a badly shaken Asian man who had witnessed army trucks piled high with bodies heading toward Lake Victoria. Amin's northern Ugandan soldiers were purging the army of its southern soldiers.

Heading home through Addis Ababa, I had a spooky unscheduled stop in Asmara, Eritrea, which was still part of Ethiopia at that point, but fighting for independence. Every time I went for a walk in the city, I was followed by squads of secret police. When I stopped for the layover in Cairo on the way home, the airport was crawling with angry Russian soldiers who had just been ordered home by President Anwar Sadat—his first move in preparation for what would become the Yom Kippur War. I arrived Beirut in time to hear that on August 4, 1972, Idi Amin had ordered the Asian community in Uganda to leave the country by November 8. My family's plan had been to take the kids camping up the coast from Beirut, passing along the Syrian coast to Turkey, but this news, coupled with two other pieces of personal news interfered with our plans. In the third week of August the embassy doctor ruled that, that because of complications with a previous pregnancy, Jo was not to have our third child in Beirut, and that she had to depart without delay for Vancouver, where she could get better care and her mother could provide support. That same day, I received a message from the Canadian national headquarters in Ottawa that I was to be in Detroit by December to open a new visa office there. This was quite surprising, as we'd been in Beirut only eight months, and postings generally lasted longer than that. As Jo and I were absorbing these developments, Roger St. Vincent called me into his office and showed me another message from Ottawa, dated August 24:

> You are not unaware of General Amin's decree to expel 80,000 Asians from Uganda accusing them of being puppets of the British government and sabotaging the economy of his country. Your mission is to proceed

to Kampala and by whatever means undertake to process without numerical limitation those Asians who meet the immigration selection criteria bearing in mind their particular plight and facilitate their departure for Canada. Your mission must be accomplished by November.[1]

In many parts of Africa, including East Africa, the term "Asian" signified people originally from the Indian subcontinent. There were significant Asian communities in Kenya and Tanzania—in Uganda, these included Gujarati Hindus (50 percent) and Ismaili Muslims (30 percent), as well as smaller communities of Sikhs, Goans, Punjabi Hindus, Ithnasharis, Boas, and Parsis. Together, the Asian community owned 80 percent of the businesses in Uganda; controlled 50 percent of the industries; and constituted 50 percent of the professionals. Their relative affluence in relation to their small number (some 60,000 to 80,000), coupled with their perceived clannishness, made them a prime target for the mercurial General Amin.

Roger told me he was leaving for Kampala immediately and, since I was now, as he put it, "a seasoned officer" after my posting in Japan and eight months in Beirut, I was to accompany him. I had known Roger for four years at that point. He had served as a fighter pilot in World War II before joining the first wave of Canadian immigration officers who were sent to Europe after the war to process displaced persons from refugee camps. I'd first met Roger in 1968, when he was coordinating the transportation of Czechoslovakian refugees to Canada. I negotiated a delay in my Ugandan departure date with Roger to give me time to break our lease, pack up our belongings, and see Jo, and my two children, Kathleen and Bill, off to London, from where they would take a connecting flight to Vancouver.

1 Roger St. Vincent, *Seven Crested Cranes* (Ottawa: Canadian Immigration Historical Society, 2012), p. viii. "Seven Crested Cranes" was the title St. Vincent gave to a detailed account of the expulsion compiled from notes he kept in a journal while he was in Kampala. His account was published by the Canadian Immigration Historical Society, but St. Vincent also included it as chapter 10 of his autobiography, "A Very Fortunate Life," a privately circulated manuscript. Both the autobiography as a whole and the "Seven Crested Cranes" chapter (pp. 195–252) are available as PDFs at https://carleton.ca/uganda-collection/seven-crested-cranes-roger-st-vincent/. (In that version, this message is reproduced on p. 204.) In what follows, I have drawn on his account as the most reliable source of statistical information.

I arrived at Entebbe Airport around noon on September 5. The driver of the white minivan with Canadian flags taped to the doors offered to take me to the Apollo International Hotel, where I was booked to stay; however, when he told me the Canadian High Commission had an office, which was news to me since there had been no office on my recent visit, I asked to go there instead. It turned out that the office was a large space in the Industrial Promotion Services Building on Kampala's main drag, and the largest office building in town. It had been vacant when Roger arrived a few days before, but it was now a hive of activity, with specially ordered office furniture coming through the door. As I looked around, I could see a number of people from Ottawa and embassies in Europe (visa officers, doctors, visa typists, clerks), as well as two diplomats on loan from the High Commission of Canada to Kenya in Nairobi. I had barely come through the door when I heard Roger shout from across the room, "Hey Molloy! Did you come to look or to work?" I dumped my bags and walked over to him. He told me we were opening to the public the next morning, September 6. Then he handed me a hand-drawn floor plan, told me to get the office set up right away, and to meet him at the hotel at 6:00 p.m.

Besides getting the office ready for business, the critical problem we had to solve before opening our doors officially was how to establish and maintain contact with those members of the Asian community in Uganda who wanted to come to Canada. Amin's deadline for their departure was November 8, which was just eight weeks away. Mail was too slow, telephones were unreliable; both were insecure. Ottawa-based clerk Jim McMaster offered the solution. He produced a little silver number-stamping machine, which, he explained, could be set to repeat a number up to nine times before moving on to the next one. We set it to stamp each number twice, once on each new application and once on a set of "tax clearance" instructions printed on the grey stationery that had been given to us in a neighbourly gesture by the British High Commission, which had an immigration team on the ground floor below us. These proved to be extremely useful, as Asians leaving permanently for the United Kingdom, Canada, and all other destinations, needed to know how to obtain a Ugandan tax clearance, which they needed before they could leave the country. Stamping the tax clearance instructions meant the paper could double as a receipt. We would communicate with applicants by putting advertisements in the local paper that contained lists of numbers and interview times. Applicants could check the receipts they had been given on application, and if their number appeared in the advertisement, they could come to the office at the time provided. Brilliant, simple, reliable, and most importantly, secure. Only the applicant knew his or her number. McMaster's stamping machine was the pivot around which our communications, file control, and applicant privacy systems revolved. I doubt we could have managed without it. Within two weeks, we started receiving offers of assistance from Canada that included these numbers.

The lineup on September 6 stretched for blocks. Three visa typists from Ottawa were assigned to the reception counter. They handed out thousands of immigration forms and by the end of the day had taken in and number-stamped 2,588 applications for a total of 7,764 people. We calculated that we needed to see at least seventy-five people a day if we wanted to process the applications on time. The first lists of the file numbers of people we needed to see appeared in the *Uganda Argus* four days later, on September 10.

THE POLICY FRAMEWORK

The framework of an actual Canadian refugee policy had been set two years before, in 1970, with a Cabinet decision to adopt the official United Nations definition of "refugee"; to use a point-based system with a generous amount of positive discretion to select refugees; and to extend Canada's resettlement activities beyond Europe. Most important in this case, the Cabinet decision introduced the "Oppressed Minority" policy.[2] By definition, refugees are people who have fled persecution and are outside their country at the time of application. The Oppressed Minority policy enabled Cabinet to authorize visa officers to apply refugee rules to oppressed people who were not technically refugees because they had not left their country. Since it was a Cabinet document, few of us at the working level of government ever saw it, but it became a key document in the evolution of Canadian refugee policy, as it opened the door to refugees from around the world. The Ugandan Asians fell into this category, since they were under an expulsion order, but still in

2 Memorandum to the Cabinet, "Selection of Refugees for Resettlement in Canada," July 27, 1970, RG 2, vol. 6373, file 1032-70, Library and Archives Canada. The content of the Cabinet decision was communicated to immigration staff in Operation Memorandum no. 17, January 2, 1971.

CANADA

CANADIAN HIGH COMMISSION
IMMIGRATION SERVICE

INTERVIEWS

I.P.S. BUILDING, KAMPALA

Holders of the following reference numbers
are invited to appear for Interview Wednesday,

Sept. 13, 8:30 to 12:00 and 2:00 to 4:00.

8.30 to 10.30	10.30 to 12.00	2.00 to 3.00	3.00 to 4.00
174			
248	398	530	622
290	409	531	623
295	410	539	624
304	411	544	625
		550	627
305	412	551	631
306	413	567	635
307	426	568	641
324	428	577	642
329	430	579	646
337	450	580	649
339	458	586	669
341	462	587	670
343	468	601	676
350	505	610	689
364	506	615	693
367	507		694
368	510		
378	511		
382	517		
397	523		

Only those heads of family or single persons whose REFERENCE NUMBERS appear above
will be interviewed. All other holders of reference
numbers will be invited through subsequent newspaper notices or contacted by mail. If you hold
a reference number please refrain from contacting this office unless invited to do so.

List of Immigration Service reference numbers issued to visa applicants.
These lists, which were published in the *Uganda Argus* starting
September 10, 1972, allowed interviewees to be notified swiftly while at
the same time protecting their privacy.

Source: Bennett Collection: The *Uganda Argus* Newspaper, in the Uganda
Collection, Carleton University Library, Archives and Special Collections, Ottawa,
https://www.carleton.ca/uganda-collection/archival-material/.

Uganda. Roger's original instructions put the emphasis on applying normal immigrant selection criteria as determined by the point system but, after Cabinet met on September 13, 1972, all subsequent communications emphasized humanitarian concerns first and foremost, paying particular attention to those who had nowhere to go. Prime Minister Trudeau's announcement of the program left us in no doubt about the approach we were to take. "For our part, we are prepared to offer an honourable place in Canadian life to those Ugandan Asians who come to Canada under this program," he said. "Asian immigrants have already added to the cultural richness and variety of our country, and I am sure that those from Uganda will, by their abilities and industry, make an equally important contribution to Canadian society."[3] On the ground in Kampala, we were unaware of any controversy surrounding the role of the Aga Khan or his representatives in the selection of refugees.

Amin's earlier pronouncement was ambiguous enough to leave the impression that only Asians who opted to keep their British colonial documents would have to leave, but that those who had taken out Ugandan citizenship might be able to stay. From our perspective in Kampala, any ambiguity about the intent of the expulsion order was resolved toward the end of September when the Ugandan government ordered a citizenship verification process that applied only to people of Asian descent. The "process" resulted in large numbers of Asian Ugandans being arbitrarily stripped of their citizenship. Since having Ugandan citizenship clearly no longer offered them protection from Amin's random shifts in policy, we were instructed to treat Asians who still had Ugandan citizenship as if they were stateless.

As the situation could change almost daily, we adopted a flexible selection policy that looked roughly like this: Those who qualified under the point system were accepted regardless of whether they held British, Indian, Pakistani, or Ugandan citizenship, or whether they were stateless or not. Those who did not qualify under the point system fell into two categories: If they were stateless or were Ugandan citizens who had nowhere else to go, they were given sympathetic consideration and were usually accepted using the visa officers' discretionary authority. Those who had permission to go to the United Kingdom or who held Indian or Pakistani citizenship were not normally called for an interview unless they had a relative or offer of assistance

3 Pierre Trudeau, "Statement from the Prime Minister," quoted in St. Vincent, *Seven Crested Cranes*, 6. (In the PDF version, see p. 205.)

from someone in Canada, or there was another compelling circumstance. People with physical disabilities were given priority.

By the third week, we had received so many offers of assistance from relatives and friends of Ugandan Asians in Canada that we had to establish special procedures to keep track of them, and we decided to accept them at face value when making selection decisions.

CHALLENGES

Three problems emerged in the first weeks of the operation. The first problem was that Cabinet had made no concessions on medical screening, which meant that all applicants were required to undergo a full "tropical" examination that included a blood test for syphilis, urinalysis, a stool examination for parasites, an X-ray for TB, and a full physical examination. Dr. Piché, head of the medical team, refused to allow the doctors to do the physical until all test results were in. By September 12, we had a medical backlog of 1,600 people waiting for exams. The Canadian Forces had been instructed by Cabinet to send a team of medical technicians to do the testing, but they arrived a week after the rest of the us and were not fully operational until September 20. Since we could not issue visas without medical clearance and the backlog was too large to handle without assistance, the first charter flight, optimistically scheduled for September 15, had to be cancelled—to NHQ in Ottawa's extreme annoyance.

The second problem was that many Asians in Uganda still hoped Amin would change his mind and were therefore reluctant to make firm departure plans. The third problem was that armed followers of deposed President Obote and Amin's opponents invaded Uganda from Tanzania. The invaders were brutally crushed within a week, but the slack Ugandan Army discipline occasioned by the fighting made travel outside Kampala dangerous, and even within the capital we heard reports of killings and terror. We got a good scare when a military convoy stopped in front of our building and all the soldiers pointed their weapons at us. We closed the office for the rest of the day and confined staff to the hotel. A belligerent Army officer appeared in the hotel dining room that night and demanded that we eat in silence.

Despite these challenges, we were able to get the first charter flight of refugees off to Canada on September 27. Our government's initial plan was to finance the charters by giving the refugees Assisted Passage Loans. When we reported that the Ugandan government was planning to tax the loans, Trudeau responded by announcing there would be no loans and that the Canadian government would cover the costs. The 20-kilometre stretch of road from Kampala to Entebbe Airport was notoriously unsafe thanks to numerous checkpoints staffed by rapacious soldiers. Consequently, we decided to hire buses that would go directly to the terminal, previously checking in our Canada-bound passengers in the parking lot of the Apollo International Hotel, where we were all staying. We draped the buses with Canadian flags, and our High Commissioner came to Kampala from Nairobi to escort the first flight's passengers to the airport. Subsequent bus convoys to the airport were led by the High Commissioner's car, flag and all, with the Nairobi-based diplomats playing the role of "His Excellency," much to the annoyance of the Ugandan foreign ministry. This was perhaps unorthodox, but it did mean that all our refugees got to the airport without being harassed or robbed.

The first flight took 30 hours, including a stopover for repairs in Paris. On arrival in Canada, the newcomers were bused to Canadian Forces Base Longue-Pointe in Montréal for rest, immigration formalities, issuance of winter clothing, and counselling regarding their destinations. On arrival, they were also served a range of Indian dishes that the Canadian Army cooks had learned to make—the food garnered rave reviews from the new arrivals. Three weeks into the program, we had received 6,355 applications, conducted 785 interviews, issued 663 visas, had 927 people in the queue for medical exams, and had scheduled 2,400 interviews for the next eleven days.

TURNING THE CORNER

On the Uganda national day weekend (October 7–9), we closed our doors and sent the junior staff and medical technicians off to Mombasa, Kenya, for a rest. At the same time, reinforcements, including more officers and visa typists, arrived from Ottawa, and over the three-day weekend we reviewed 6,000 applications, looking particularly for stateless people and those with no obvious place to go. The review identified applications we had previously passed over because the applicants were Ugandan citizens who did not qualify under the point system before we were instructed to consider them as stateless. We scheduled 1,988 for interviews at the rate of 145 a day up to the end of October, while the newly arrived typists banged out another 656 visas.

By this time, the Kampala team had evolved into four distinct but closely linked units. I supervised the selection unit comprising visa officers who screened applications and conducted selection interviews. Sergeant John Stronach led a team of seven military medical technicians who analyzed medical samples. Dr. Marcel Piché from the Department of Health and Welfare managed a unit of four or five doctors who conducted physical examinations and rendered medical decisions.[4] Gerry Campbell, a newcomer to the immigration foreign service, was in charge of the Visa Transportation Unit, which managed the files, produced the visas, assembled passenger manifests, and saw the refugees safely to the airport and onto the chartered flights.

Over the next few weeks, the rate of charter departures increased from three a week to at least one a day. At one point, a Canadian professor from Makerere University in Kampala asked if we could do anything for twenty Asian medical students who had been dismissed from the university. Recalling how Canada had taken in the entire faculty and staff of Hungary's Sophoron Forestry School in 1956–57, I suggested he contact the head of the Association of Universities and Colleges of Canada (AUCC) to see whether they could help. Two days later, he reappeared with a telegram from the AUCC president that said essentially, "You send them, we'll place them." There was no space for them on our interview schedule, so Roger St. Vincent agreed that I could see them the coming weekend. I deputized the professor to assist me and interviewed the students five at a time that Sunday. All but one, who went to the UK, proceeded to Canada and careers in the medical field.

THE MAN, THE GUN, AND THE CHAIN

An incident that sticks with me took place the second or third week of October. I was on my fourth or fifth interview of the morning when Maurice ("Mo") Benoit, our front-counter man, suddenly interrupted, telling me there was someone I needed to see right away. He was back within seconds with an application form and accompanied by a large Ugandan police sergeant. I was surprised to see the sergeant and shocked to see that he had a submachine gun in one hand and a chain in the other with a smallish, dishevelled Asian man handcuffed to the end of the chain. The man croaked "You called my number" and handed me a battered piece of grey British High Commission

---

4 The number of staff on the ground varied daily as people arrived and left to return to Canada as their availability allowed. As a result, it is difficult to pin down exact numbers for any of these teams.

stationery with a number that matched the one on the application Mo had just handed me. The sergeant declined to remove the cuffs, so I put his chair behind the man's so we could have a whispered conversation.

He explained that the previous week Amin had ordered Asians with Kenyan, Tanzanian, and Zambian passports to leave the country. His wife had a Kenyan passport, so they decided she would join her parents in Kenya and await the outcome of his Canadian application. At the border, the Ugandan authorities seized her jewellery, expelled her to Kenya, charged him with smuggling, and sent him to the notorious Kampala jail. His family was unsuccessful in getting him released until his number appeared in the *Uganda Argus* and they persuaded the warden to let him attend his interview. He was clearly an "oppressed minority," and his application revealed that he was a mechanic (maximum points) with an aunt in BC (more points), so I did not even have to use my discretionary authority to approve his application.

Next stop was the medical section, where the normally prickly Dr. Piché greeted us with a smile and disappeared with the man, chain still attached, behind the curtain while the sergeant and I compared his World War II service in Burma with my Dad's in the North Atlantic. Dr. Piché reappeared and announced the man with the chain had passed the medical examination (clearly without any of the prerequisite X-ray, or blood, urine, or stool tests). Then Roger St. Vincent appeared out of nowhere in his usual military-cut safari suit, planted himself in front of the sergeant, and informed him, with his authoritative RCAF flight lieutenant voice, that the man was to be delivered to Entebbe Airport the next morning at precisely 7:00 a.m. It was a solid rendition of the "Was that understood? Yes sir. Very good, make it so. Yes sir" routine. Then Dr. Piché, clearly still oozing good will, told the sergeant that if all went well, he could bring his family to the office the following day for a free medical examination.

The next morning at 7:00, several police cars drove across the tarmac to where an Air Canada passenger jet was waiting. Roger was waiting at the top of the stairs. The sergeant, minus machine gun but with man and chain, came up the stairs. Roger ordered the handcuffs removed before shoving the man through the door. The sergeant asked if he could look inside the plane. Roger politely declined but told him he was looking forward to meeting him and his family the following day.

The following morning, the sergeant, accompanied by his wife and six children, appeared at the counter at our Kampala headquarters. Dr. Piché, our volunteer nurses, and the other doctors ensured that they were treated like royalty, fed them tea and biscuits, and after a thorough medical examination, sent them on their way with a bag of medical supplies and a certificate of good health.

THE FINAL PHASE

As the deadline for expulsion grew near, fewer people appeared for interview: on the last interview day, October 31, we interviewed 59 people even though we had invited 132. Between October 28 and November 8, we sent twelve charter flights to Canada and quietly dismantled our facility, donated the furniture to a UN operation that was starting up next door, and sent team members home in small groups. In the end, we had issued visas for 6,292 persons (2,115 cases). Of these visas, 117 were never claimed, leaving an effective total of 6,175 people, of whom 4,420 travelled on the thirty-one charter flights we had arranged and another 1,725 made their own way to Canada. A surprising number of people, mainly from smaller remote towns, made no attempt to apply for resettlement and ended up in refugee camps in Europe. Canada accepted approximately two thousand of these over the next two years.

Mo Benoit and I were the last of the team to leave Kampala. Roger had asked me to remain in Nairobi for an extra week to deal with any Ugandans stranded there, which I did. I made it back to Beirut by mid-November, where I received instructions to proceed to Ottawa for my new assignment in Buffalo (not Detroit). After a month on the equator, Ottawa seemed very cold. Once there, I learned I was to open a visa office in Minneapolis (not Buffalo) on December 4, after which I was free to go to Vancouver. I arrived in Vancouver in time to take Jo to the hospital for the birth of our daughter, Tara (mother and beautiful daughter were fine), and stayed long enough to bring her to our temporary home there before returning to Minneapolis. It was another six weeks before we were back together.

IMPACT

Following the 1970 Cabinet decision to extend Canada's resettlement program beyond Europe, there had been efforts to move small numbers of

Tibetan and Chinese refugees from Hong Kong, but the Ugandan Asian exercise was the first real test of the new policy. The Prime Minister's prediction that "those from Uganda will, by their abilities and industry, make an equally important contribution to Canadian society" turned out to be an understatement. The original Ugandans and their children can be found across the country and in all walks of life, in business, public service, education, the justice system, the media, the arts, and politics. The values of public service and volunteerism they brought with them have made them a particularly valuable component of our society.

Four years later (1976), I was back in Ottawa as the director of refugee policy, leading a small team responsible for implementing the many refugee provisions of the 1976 Immigration Act. The Uganda experience drove home the reality that not everyone who needs resettlement is a refugee as defined by the UN Refugee Convention. It convinced me of the usefulness of tailoring our refugee resettlement definitions to the characteristics of the people we were trying to help. This, in turn, informed the decisions we made in crafting the various designated classes—such as Indochinese, Political Prisoners, Oppressed Persons, and Self-Exiled—that shaped our resettlement program for the next two decades. When it came time to instruct the team that designed the sponsorship program, I told them about the psychological relief I felt when I opened an application in the midst of the Kampala pressure cooker to find a message from someone in Canada who cared for the person who was sitting in front of me. That simple message had eased the decision-making process immeasurably. As we completed the design of the sponsorship system in the spring of 1978, a young man stomped into my office and demanded to know why we didn't have a program for refugee students. I told him it was because no one had asked for one, and then told him about the medical students in Kampala. A couple of months later, we signed a refugee student sponsorship agreement with World University Service of Canada. Though we could not know it at the time, the Uganda operation in 1972 served as a dress rehearsal for the massive Indochinese refugee program that brought sixty thousand Vietnamese, Cambodian, and Laotian refugees to Canada in 1979–80. By that time, the lessons learned in Kampala had been absorbed into the legislative (1976) and regulatory (1978) frameworks, and line officers who learned their business under St. Vincent in Kampala played leadership roles in both Southeast Asia and at immigration headquarters.

Reflecting on the Role of
the Mennonite Central Committee in
Advocating for Refugees

WILLIAM JANZEN

Advocating for refugees in Canada can make a difference in many ways. In this account I will concentrate on the refugee advocacy work I did in my job as the director of the Ottawa Office of Mennonite Central Committee (MCC). That position, which I was privileged to hold from 1975 to 2008, involved advocacy work on many issues, reflecting MCC's broad involvement in international relief, development and peacebuilding, but at times I had to focus on refugee issues in a particular way.

Refugee work has a notable place in Mennonite history. In the 1920s, Mennonite churches in Canada helped some 21,000 Mennonites in Russia to escape the violence relating to the Communist revolution and resettle in Canada. After World War II, the MCC resettled thousands more, some in Canada and others elsewhere. Through the MCC, which was founded in 1920, Mennonites have done refugee relief work in many places around the world. The Mennonite experience of being refugees in the sixteenth and seventeenth centuries, when they were severely persecuted, as well as the practical emphasis of their theology, have also helped to nurture a certain readiness to assist refugees.

My first major advocacy initiative on refugees involved negotiating, early in 1979, Canada's first "master agreement" for the private sponsorship of refugees. The context was that the media, since the fall of 1978, had reported extensively on the tens of thousands of people who were fleeing Vietnam. These refugees had set out in small boats in the hope of getting temporary refuge in Thailand, Malaysia, Indonesia, or other neighbouring countries, and eventually being permanently resettled somewhere. These "boat people" as they were referred to took great risks. An untold number drowned at sea; others were raped and robbed by pirates; and neighbouring countries, afraid of being flooded with people, began to turn them away, leaving them adrift on the sea.

Although Canada was far away, people here wanted to help. Many called on the federal government to bring over some of these refugees. Others wanted to take steps on their own. With that in mind, my MCC superiors instructed me to approach officials at what was then the department of employment and immigration to work out an arrangement so that Mennonite churches in Canada could bring people over and help them to build new lives here. I called Calbert Best, the assistant deputy minister for immigration, with whom I had recently worked on other issues. Cal was remarkably receptive. The 1976 Immigration Act, which had come into force in 1978, included a provision for the private sponsorship of refugees. He told me that he and his officials had been thinking about how to activate that provision.

We quickly convened a meeting with Best and other officials, at which I was joined by several MCC colleagues from our head office in Winnipeg. The new immigration law enabled the sponsorship not only of Convention refugees (that is, individuals who meet the criteria of the UN Convention Relating to the Status of Refugees) but also of members of "designated classes" of refugees—groups designated as refugees on humanitarian grounds. The officials explained how the new law's "designated class" provision gave them greater flexibility when it came to sponsorship agreements. We then talked about an agreement in broad terms, after which Gordon Barnett, from the government's side, and I, from MCC's side, were seconded to flesh out the agreement and write it up.

Gordon and I met several times over the next few weeks following that initial meeting, always checking with our respective colleagues. Both sides were eager to move forward, so the negotiations proceeded well. As Gordon later explained, he was originally instructed to aim for a clear line of separation between the private sponsorship program and the government's existing resettlement programs, but "as negotiations progressed and the goodwill of MCC became evident," this approach was abandoned: "Bill [Janzen] negotiated in such good faith, it was embarrassing to play the cards I had been given . . . . Negotiating with MCC demonstrated only their complete commitment to help, against our reluctance to give anything up and our meanness. I thought we should adopt a different, more cooperative approach." As he went on to say, "It may well be that had the first agreement not been negotiated with a group as openly altruistic and sincerely helpful as MCC, the National Sponsorship Agreements would have been less cooperative."[1] On March 5, 1979, our executive director, J. M. Klassen, and the Honourable Bud Cullen, then the minister of employment and immigration, signed a master agreement (MA). It was the first of its kind, and it led to extensive private sponsorship, which then became a hallmark of Canadian refugee policy.

The essence of the MA was simple. The requirement in the law was that if five Canadians wanted to sponsor a refugee, they had to accept full liability for one year. This had made people hesitate as they imagined worst-case scenarios. With the MA, MCC as a national organization accepted full liability, while any congregation or group of people whom MCC authorized would do the actual work. Thus, small church groups would carry all the normal settlement costs, but they would not be left liable if exceptional problems developed. In addition to accepting liability, MCC provided counsel, guidance, and general coordination. For their part, government officials had confidence that MCC and any groups it authorized would carry through.

It was also agreed that refugees sponsored by private groups would not be counted toward the government's own target number; they would be over and above those sponsored by the government. The government would assist private groups with language training services. Also, alongside the sponsorship track, there was a "joint assistance" track for special-needs cases. For these, the government would provide private groups with additional resources and they would then be counted as "government-sponsored." The

---

1 Barnett's comments are quoted in Michael J. Molloy, Peter Duschinsky, Kurt F. Jensen, and Robert J. Shalka, *Running on Empty: Canada and the Indochinese Refugee Crisis, 1975–1980* (Montréal and Kingston: McGill-Queen's University Press, 2017), 76–77.

MA also outlined the flow of communications—for example, from MCC to a church group anywhere in Canada, to a local immigration office, to immigration headquarters in Ottawa, to the embassies in Southeast Asia, indicating what was to happen at each stage.

Soon after MCC signed the MA, a majority of the six hundred Mennonite congregations in Canada submitted applications to sponsor refugees. And in the next weeks and months, twenty-eight other national church bodies and dioceses signed virtually identical agreements with the department of employment and immigration. In June 1979, Howard Adelman, a professor at the University of Toronto, founded Operation Lifeline, and, in July, Ottawa's mayor, Marion Dewar, launched Project 4000. In a subsequent memorandum to the Cabinet regarding the Indochinese refugee situation, Minister Ron Atkey (who had replaced Bud Cullen) noted that "both the volume and pace of sponsorship commitments exceeded the most optimistic expectations."[2] This unexpected response led the newly elected government of Joe Clark to vastly increase the number of refugees that the country would admit, despite an ambivalence in public opinion. As recently as June 1979, Canada had been planning for a total of 12,000 Indochinese refugees—8,000 sponsored by the government and the other 4,000 privately. But, in late July, Flora MacDonald, the minister of external affairs, supported by Prime Minister Joe Clark, raised the total number to 50,000. The target for privately sponsored refugees was raised to 21,000, and the government committed to matching this figure (in addition to the 8,000 government sponsorships already in process). Altogether, from 1975 to the end of 1980, Canada took in 70,000 refugees from Indochina, approximately one-half of them privately sponsored.

As the authors of the 2017 study, *Running on Empty: Canada and the Indochinese Refugee Crisis, 1975–1980*, observe, Canada's private sponsorship program "has been frequently examined by other governments seeking to strengthen their resettlement programs, but it has not been easy to transplant it elsewhere, less because of its design than because of the value system that underpins it."[3] But has that underlying value system remained strong? Canada's churches, who did most of the sponsoring in 1979–80, are weaker

2 Quoted in ibid., 155. The memorandum (PCO 693-79MC) was titled "Indochinese Refugees" and dated November 13, 1979.

3 Ibid., 81.

now. The general feeling about being able to make a difference in the world has declined. Increased security concerns have coloured the perception of refugees. As a result, there is less pressure on the government to open doors. Nevertheless, churches and other groups continue to sponsor refugees under the private sponsorship umbrella.

My second significant involvement with refugees took place in 1987. This time it was not about sponsoring refugees from distant camps. Rather, it had to do with people who came to a Canadian point of entry and claimed to be refugees, defined by the 1951 UN Refugee Convention as people who have a "well-founded fear of being persecuted for reasons of race, religion, nationality, membership of a particular social group or political opinion." When Canada finally ratified the Convention in 1969, the government committed itself to granting a fair hearing to people who had made their way to Canada and claimed to be refugees.

Until this time, the question of how to give a hearing to such people was not a big issue because Canada, being far away from areas that had many refugees, received few refugee claims. But in 1981 there were 1,600 such claims, averaging 133 per month, and in 1987 there were 2,000 per month, partly because of civil wars in Central America. In 1985 the Supreme Court's ruling in *Singh v. Minister of Employment and Immigration* had reinforced the importance of giving hearings to refugee claimants.[4] But to do that called for a substantial administrative/judicial structure. Since Canada did not have such a structure in place, a huge backlog had built up, that is, people who had been allowed into Canada while they waited for a hearing. Eventually, many of these people would be allowed to stay, but the increase meant a new system was needed to manage applications.

Then in the summer of 1987, a boatload of Sikhs arrived in Nova Scotia. Prime Minister Mulroney recalled Parliament for an emergency session and brought in legislation concerning refugees. The bill in question, Bill C-55, would set up a judicial structure, the Immigration and Refugee Board (IRB). While giving the Board authority to deal with refugees, it also limited access to the IRB. One way of doing this was that the bill gave the government the power to designate a country as "a safe third country." This meant that a

---

4 *Singh v. Minister of Employment and Immigration*, 1985 CanLII 65 (SCC), [1985] 1 SCR 177, https://www.canlii.org/en/ca/scc/doc/1985/1985canlii65/1985canlii65.html.

person who came to Canada via such a country would not have a right to a hearing in Canada. This step was related to similar moves in other Western countries. There was a joint desire to ensure that claimants, if they had had a hearing in one country and had been refused there, would not be able to get a hearing in another, and another.

This legislation led to considerable public debate that summer. A number of refugee support groups appeared before a Parliamentary Committee, and some of the sessions were acrimonious. To prepare for MCC's appearance before the Parliamentary Committee on September 2, I worked closely with Stuart Clark, MCC's Refugee Coordinator. We invited David Janzen, the coordinator of our "Overground Railroad" in the United States, and Carmen Albrecht, who had served with MCC in Guatemala for three years and who was now working with a refugee program in Kitchener, to join us.

In our presentation to the Parliamentary Committee, we reviewed MCC's refugee work in general and then focused on our current involvement with people from Central America who had fled to the United States. Since their chances of being given refugee status in the United States were very slim, our partners in the United States had helped many to apply at Canadian consulates in the United States where, we were pleased to report, Canadian officials had proven quite sympathetic. We also described cases where people, for various reasons, could not apply through the consulates; they needed to get to a Canadian entry point, make an "inland claim," and get a hearing. Then we pointed out how aspects of the proposed legislation could prevent such people from getting a hearing. We were able to describe the situation of actual people rather than talk about principles and laws in the abstract. It seemed that the MPs were moved by our stories of people. Also, we could show that we preferred to see refugees apply through consulates and embassies abroad, just as the government did, while pointing out that for some people, getting to a Canadian entry point and making an inland claim was the only option and that certain aspects of the proposed legislation could prevent them from getting here.

Soon after our appearance before the committee, I received two letters of appreciation. One was from a government MP who, by reputation, was the most hard-hearted defender of the legislation. The other was from an Opposition MP who said that after our presentation the government MP had become remarkably sympathetic. The Opposition MP felt that by describing our hands-on work, expressing appreciation for officials, detailing how actual individuals would be affected if all aspects of this legislation were implemented, and remaining moderate in our requests, we had helped the Committee to look at the legislation in a more humane way. The fact that all the reporters were covering an appearance of former Prime Minister Pierre Trudeau elsewhere on Parliament Hill that evening may also have been helped to give our session a non-partisan atmosphere.

A third round of advocacy work took place in 1992. The issues were similar to those of 1987. People from Central America were continuing to flee north. The number of annual claimants had risen to 30,000 and it was costly for the Immigration and Refugee Board (IRB) to hear so many cases. In an effort to restrict access to the IRB, the government proposed giving Senior Immigration Officers the authority to bar people from getting to the IRB if they came via a "prescribed" country, meaning a safe third country, or from a country of origin presumed to be safe. The bill also required that to get a hearing, claimants had to come with valid passports or other travel documents. People with a criminal record could also be barred.

I asked for an opportunity to appear before the Senate Committee studying the bill. To prepare, I contacted people who were directly involved with refugees: Rudy Baergen, senior minister at First Mennonite Church in Kitchener, Betty Puricelli, from the New Life Centre in Toronto, and John Doherty from the Mennonite House of Friendship in Montréal. They joined me before the Senate Committee on September 4, 1992. The title of our 16-page brief was, "Love the Sojourner . . . for You Were Sojourners" (Deuteronomy 10:19).

These three individuals provided ten stories of refugees with whom they had been involved. On that basis, we then questioned several elements in the bill. Regarding the "safe third country" concept, we argued that many refugees would be at the mercy of the seriously inadequate system in the United States. Regarding the requirement that refugees come with proper documentation, we said that for many an attempt to get passports from their own governments would be to risk their lives. Regarding the exclusion of anyone believed to have been convicted of a crime, we asked whether this meant that Canadian authorities would get such information from the home government from which the person was fleeing. We also requested a procedure to appeal IRB rulings. We acknowledged that the number of claimants had risen substantially but noted that it was still well below that of many other refugee-receiving countries.

I do not recall details of the outcome, but I do remember the Senate Committee listening attentively and asking good questions. My next report to my board stated: "The Senate Committee's report, released in mid-September, reflected many of the concerns that we and other groups raised." In 2002, the government did enter into a Safe Third Country Agreement (STCA) with the United States, which came into effect in 2004. There were qualifications such as a claimant needing to have family members in Canada, but the Canadian Council for Refugees (CCR), joined by the Canadian Council of Churches and Amnesty International, soon began an effort to have the agreement rescinded, arguing persuasively that for many refugee claimants it was not possible to get a fair hearing in the United States. That effort continued, and in July 2020 the Federal Court found that that agreement with the United States violated the Canadian Charter of Rights and Freedoms.

Interestingly, the Canada-United States Safe Third Country Agreement applies only at official ports of entry into Canada. It does not apply to people who walk across the border from the United States into Canada at some other place, as many have done in recent years, nor to people once they are in Canada. In 2010, the government brought in legislation to create a Designated Countries of Origin list, meaning countries where conditions are believed to be such that people need not become refugees. If people from such countries come to Canada and make a claim, they can still appear before the IRB, but in a more circumscribed way.

Over the years I also made many appeals on behalf of individual refugees. Usually this meant getting details about the dangers that they had personally faced, some of which were horrific. In some cases, I would write this up with as much supportive documentation as I could find and then give it to a lawyer for presentation to the IRB. At other times it involved appealing to the minister on the "humanitarian and compassionate" grounds that are provided in the law. One such case, in 2006, involved a young Muslim man from Turkey who had gone to the United States to study and then, after doing so, had come to Canada as a conscientious objector. Until then I did not know that there was a small stream in Islamic thought that favoured conscientious objection. This young man's conscientious objector views had also been influenced by his Mennonite roommate at that American university.

Unfortunately, Turkey's laws did not protect conscientious objectors. Military service was compulsory and people who refused, as Jehovah's Witnesses and some others did, were usually given two-year prison sentences. If the individuals still refused, these sentences were imposed again and again. Understandably, this young man did not want to go back to Turkey. But to stay in the United States was problematic since he only had a student visa there. Given these factors, he came to Canada and asked for refugee status. But the IRB refused his claim, as did the Federal Appeal Court. Their reasoning was that to be prosecuted for refusing to serve in the military did not constitute persecution as defined by the UN Refugee Convention and that the law requiring military service was of general application and could therefore not be said to violate any one person's rights.

I submitted a substantial letter to the minister of citizenship and immigration, Monte Solberg, on this young man's behalf, supplementing my letter with a submission from his lawyer. In my letter, I reviewed the history of conscientious objector laws in Canada, which date back to 1793 and the first Assembly of Upper Canada and recounted the experience of Canadian conscientious objectors in the two World Wars. Then I described the post–World War II trend in Western countries to accept conscientious objection as a "right." I referred to formal steps taken by the European Parliament and by the United Nations Commission for Human Rights and to changes made in the International Covenant on Civil and Political Rights. I also referred to the Canadian Charter of Rights and Freedoms and to a letter I received in 1981 from Jean Chrétien, then minister of justice, when the Charter was being formulated, and in which he held that the Charter's freedom of conscience provision was sufficiently broad to cover conscientious objection.

After making that appeal to the immigration minister, we waited for over a year. During that time, this young Muslim man often came to our office. He was anxious, asking if there was anything more we could do to ensure a favourable decision and what to do if the decision went against him. Late in 2007, he received a notice asking him to come to one government office at a certain time to pick up an envelope containing the minister's decision. Being nervous, he asked me to go with him. I will never forget his relief when we read the letter and learned that he would be allowed to stay. The letter also suggested that our submission had been helpful. Not long thereafter that young man enrolled in law school and became a lawyer working for the government.

I was also able to help certain Mennonites. Technically they were not refugees, but they had some refugee characteristics. They are the descendants of the six thousand conservative Mennonites who, in the 1920s, moved from Manitoba and Saskatchewan to Mexico. The governments in these provinces, in the fervently patriotic climate after World War I, began to force them to send their children to English-language public schools. Until then they had been allowed to have their own church-run schools in the German language. Determined to resist assimilation into Canadian society, they then moved to Mexico, where they were allowed to again live more by themselves, separate from the larger society.

For some of these Mennonites, however, things did not work out, in part because their strict religious teachings restricted their economic options. Poverty became a serious problem for quite a few of them. As well, there were security issues. As a result, there was a steady trickle of migrants returning to Canada. For several decades this was quite easy because those people born in Canada still had Canadian citizenship and because others could easily get landed immigrant status. But by the 1970s, Canada's immigration laws were narrowing significantly. Soon after I started in the MCC Ottawa Office in 1975, I was asked to explore whether the fact that these people were of Canadian ancestry might open some doors under Canada's citizenship laws.

These efforts led to changes in certain citizenship policies that, in the following decades, enabled a significant portion of those in Mexico to regain Canadian citizenship. Exact numbers are not available, but a recent survey of the workers involved leads me to believe that some 85,000 people received Canadian citizenship certificates in this way. Most of these then moved to the southern areas of Ontario, Manitoba, and Alberta, where agricultural jobs were readily available. During the decades of this migration, I kept in close contact with officials in Ottawa on various legal aspects and made sure that the "documentation workers" in Mexico and in different parts of Canada had up-to-date information about the relevant laws and procedures. One criticism of this work was that it was so focused on Mennonites of Canadian background. My response was that I would have been just as happy to help Hispanic Mexicans but that in this situation the laws were such that we could help only those of Canadian ancestry.

While the work described above was related to my job, I have also done considerable refugee work on a personal volunteer basis. This has involved such mundane tasks as getting refugee children registered for sports teams, swimming lessons, and special classes and then providing the necessary transportation, week after week. Sometimes it has meant advocating for them at school. It has also meant explaining the importance of health cards and car insurance and the need to avoid the enticements of advertising, and helping people to untangle themselves from difficult situations as, for example, when a single mother purchased a nearly new minivan by taking out a loan at 31 percent interest, only to discover that she could not possibly keep up with the payments. Particularly difficult is when a refugee who has come to trust you asks pleadingly, "Can't you also bring over my sister and her family who have been stuck in a refugee camp in . . . for ten years?" Despite the challenges, there is much joy in seeing refugees benefit from the opportunities here and finding their way in Canadian society.

In general, I feel privileged to have been involved with refugees in these various ways. Many have made their way as skilled workers, businesspeople, or professionals, while also holding onto parts of their own traditions, thus making both economic and cultural contributions to Canada. But we should recognize that those who have been able to come to Canada and in whose lives we have been privileged to share are only a small fraction of the total. There are millions of refugees stuck in camps in Asia, Africa, and the Middle East. They survive largely because of international organizations like the United Nations High Commission for Refugees, the World Food Program, the Red Cross, and others. Canadian governments, to their credit, have long provided significant funding for these international organizations. But life in these camps is a minimal existence, with insecurity, dangers of various kinds, and an uncertain future. And even if the main resettlement countries— Canada, the United States, Australia, and several in Western Europe—were to increase their refugee intake vastly, it would still represent only a fraction of the refugee population in the camps. Eventually, the vast majority of these people will either go back to the countries they came from despite the dangers that first led them to flee, or become integrated into the countries where they have found temporary asylum. I feel that we ought to do much more to urge our government to work for refugee solutions and to seek peace and justice so that people will not become refugees in the first place.

Operation Lifeline

HOWARD ADELMAN

I had been the president of the University of Toronto chapter of the Combined Universities Campaign for Nuclear Disarmament (CUCND) in the early sixties. Though the head office of the CUCND was located in Montréal, where national policies and priorities were determined and where the core literature was published, the Toronto chapter turned out to be the largest in terms of membership, the richest in terms of finances, and the most active in terms of programs. Less than twenty years later, my experience at CUCND was transferred to the organization and activities of Operation Lifeline, which became the largest NGO fostering the private sponsorship of Indochinese refugees into Canada. One form of mobilization begat another.

Private sponsorship of refugees was an idea first initiated by Joseph Kage of the Jewish Immigrant Aid Society when he commented on Canada's 1967 white paper on immigration.[1] Kage upped his efforts in light of the plight of Soviet Jews in the 1970s and argued that Canada should insert a provision for private sponsorship in the envisioned new Immigration Act so that

---

1 Joseph Kage, "Re-appraising the Canadian Immigration Policy: An Analysis and Comments on the White Paper on Immigration," Jewish Immigrant Aid Society, January 1967.

Jewish groups and synagogues could sponsor immigration to Canada.[2] The direct result of that initiative was the inclusion in the 1976 Immigration Act, promulgated in 1978, of a small paragraph that permitted Canadian citizens in groups of at least five to privately sponsor refugees within a quota established by the government. These Sponsorship Agreement Holders, as they were called, guaranteed lodging and food, settlement assistance, and financial support for up to a year as needed.

Operation Lifeline started in the living room of my home in Toronto on June 10, 1979. By the end of that month, there were an astonishing sixty-six chapters of OL across Canada, the largest by far of any non-religiously based refugee assistance organization to emerge in response to the new legislation. The Mennonites and the Christian Reformed Church had already been organizing private sponsorships for three months. In Ottawa, Mayor Marion Dewar led Project 4000. London, Ontario had a separate movement that had arisen at the same time. Mayor Bert Weeks of Windsor organized a consortium of faith and civil society groups to assist in the integration of Indochinese refugees. The first meeting of the London consortium was held in March 1978, a year before even the Mennonite sponsorship initiative.[3] However, the founders of OL were ignorant of these earlier initiatives and were not influenced by them.

Canadian policy under the Liberal government had targeted 5,000 government-sponsored Indochinese refugees for admission into Canada for 1979. In the latter part of June, that target was raised to 12,000. Of that total, 4,000 were projected to be sponsored by the private sector. On July 18, three days before a UNHCR-led conference on refugees in Geneva, the Canadian minister of external affairs, Flora MacDonald, upped the target to 50,000, including up to 21,000 additional government sponsorships on a matching basis of one-to-one for every refugee sponsored by the private sector.[4]

The private sector exceeded its target by 50 percent. Over the next forty years, about 200,000 refugees in total were brought to Canada under the

2 Joseph Kage, "Stepping Stones Towards the New Canadian Immigration Act," *Jewish Immigrant Aid Society Information Bulletin* no. 347, November 20, 1973.

3 Giovana Roma, "The Indochinese Refugee Movement: An Exploratory Case Study of the Windsor Experience," *Refuge* 32, no. 2 (2016): 81–89.

4 For a far more detailed account, cf. Michael J. Molloy, Peter Duschinsky, Kurt F. Jensen, and Robert J. Shalka, *Running on Empty: Canada and the Indochinese Refugees, 1975–1980* (Montréal and Kingston: McGill-Queen's University Press, 2017).

private sponsorship program. The activism of the private sector created a legacy for the future in addition to helping the Indochinese refugees; OL played a significant role in that success. In July 1979, OL's offices moved from my house into a set of offices provided by Toronto Mayor John Sewell in City Hall. In August, OL moved to occupy a full floor in an old government office building. Many of the reasons for this rapid growth were serendipitous, but the most important was political. Joe Clark had just formed a Progressive Conservative minority government. When Ron Atkey was named minister of employment and immigration in the Clark government, Bud Cullen, the departing Liberal minister, briefed him on the portfolio and told him that his biggest and most immediate challenge would be dealing with the Indochinese refugee crisis. It was evident that any progressive policy toward the Indochinese refugees would enjoy all-party support. As far as OL was concerned, it was significant that Ron Atkey happened to be the member of Parliament for St. Paul's, the riding in which OL was founded.

A second favourable circumstance was that the senior civil servants who had been preparing the groundwork since the 1978 provision for private sponsorship were ready with policies and procedures, and with the paperwork and the personnel, to make private sponsorship work. These mandarins had actively been seeking private sponsorships from the faith communities. In 1979, they finally had a positive response, first from the Mennonites and then from the Christian Reformed Church.

The mandarins and the politicians were not only all onside, but together they were passionate about the project. Ron Atkey had read a recent article by Irving Abella and Harold (Hesh) Troper on the shameful actions of Canadian authorities toward Jewish refugees from Nazi Germany.[5] He did not want to go down in history as a second Frederick Blair, the director of the immigration branch of the department of mines and resources who in 1938 did his utmost to exclude Jews from entering Canada. Upon instructions from Ron Atkey, André Pilon (Citizenship and Immigration Canada's settlement director for the Ontario region) and Bob Parkes, his communications director, showed up at my house (to our surprise, if not shock because it was a Sunday and the meeting had just been organized on Friday) while our

---

5 Irving Abella and Harold Troper, "'The line must be drawn somewhere': Canada and Jewish Refugees, 1938–1939," *Canadian Historical Review* 60, no. 2 (June 1979): 178–209.

founding meeting of priests, rabbis, ministers, and friends was crafting a letter asking that Ron Atkey do more to help the refugees. André and Bob asked if they could sit in, and we agreed that they could. As we debated the wording of the letter, André asked for permission to speak and make a suggestion. Everyone assented. They informed us about the provision for private sponsorship and suggested that we might want to give witness to our convictions. We agreed, and in no time at all, had decided to set a target of fifty sponsorships for St. Paul's riding.

There was another serendipitous event that occurred at the same time. One of my graduate students who had attended the meeting turned out to be a stringer for the *Globe and Mail*. He fed the story to Dick Beddoes, whose page-long column reported a version of what we had decided to do. I only learned about this when a woman phoned me at 6:30 a.m. from Marystown, Newfoundland, on Monday morning and asked if she could help Operation Lifeline. I asked her what she was referring to. She read the *Globe's* story to me over the phone. Dick Beddoes had christened us with that name. He had also printed my name and number at the bottom of the column. The phone literally did not stop ringing for weeks. I asked the woman to organize a chapter of OL in Marystown in the same way we had done. I would send her follow-up material on how to implement a private sponsorship. This process was repeated numerous times as individuals from across the country phoned in. I told them to start a chapter or, if someone from that riding had already phoned, to get in touch with that person. The media proved to be as important as the government in pushing private sponsorships, though they had an unfortunate and mistaken habit of insisting that government policy was only a response to the pressure of the private sector.

Besides the willingness of civil society, the commitments and actions of both politicians and civil servants in the government, and the tremendous and continuous coverage by the media, there was a fourth element that contributed to OL's success. An old colleague from graduate school, now a lawyer, dropped over to the house when he could not reach me by phone. Earlier that year, he had been unsuccessful in getting his United Church to sponsor refugees. In the process, he had collected all the requisite information. Overnight, we prepared a 62-page handbook on private sponsorship, which we sent out as new chapters were organized. Mastery of facts, policies, laws, and procedures, as we had learned in the early sixties, was critical to success. By now, we had the knowledge.

We had the opportunity. We had politicians, civil servants, and major media on the same side. But what about money? On the first morning, three former Ugandan Ismaili refugees were at the front door with loads of bills—ones, fives, tens, twenties, fifties, and even hundreds. They offered the money to us to assist us in our efforts. We refused the money and insisted that they use it to start their own private sponsorship group—which they did.

With help from governments at all levels, as well as donations of time, services, and office materials, we had managed to get along without raising any money. However, Murray Koffler, a well-known philanthropist, and founder of Shoppers Drug Mart, agreed to join our board. Against my view, which was to avoid becoming a recipient of money ourselves and to insist that money be directly spent to help refugees by sponsors, Murray insisted that I was being short-sighted. Public enthusiasm would erode. New needs would emerge. Some sponsorships would run into trouble and need additional support. He proved to be correct on all three counts. With the approval of the Board and my abstention, he agreed to lead a fundraising effort. With the help of a funding marathon on the CBC that he organized and donations from other sources, he managed to raise almost $400,000, which proved to be needed, as he had anticipated.

Decades later I became involved in the attempt to get the Canadian government, first under Stephen Harper and later under Justin Trudeau, involved in expanding the program to assist Syrian refugees. I also became marginally involved in the private sponsorship of Syrian refugees through my synagogue and the beginning of Lifeline Syria. My experiences in the second decade of the twenty-first century were markedly different from those in 1979.

It helped that this time round, Mike Molloy and Naomi Alboim, both from the government policy and delivery side, and I from the private sponsorship side, were veterans of the Indochinese refugee movement. All three of us had carried out research on refugees. We were concerned with the enormous increase in Syrian refugees resulting from the Syrian civil war. Refugees were flooding into Turkey, Jordan, and Lebanon and, unlike Southeast Asia, these host countries, while troubled by the enormous responsibilities refugees thrust upon them, did not close their borders. They also had a much greater refugee burden—four million or more.

As we strategized our approach, Naomi pointed out that over the past decade, Canada had greatly increased the number of unskilled temporary workers it was bringing into the country, and that the program was fraught with difficulties. This led her to suggest that refugees could substitute for these unskilled workers. We therefore proposed greatly increasing the intake of Syrian refugees with the support of private sponsorships by arranging jobs in advance that would normally be filled by unskilled temporary guest workers. We ran two pilot workshops, one in Halifax and one in Calgary, to test the idea, not only with refugee private sponsors and settlement organizations, but also with business leaders. The idea received enthusiastic support, especially from businesses, who resented the money they spent on recruiting temporary guest workers and the loss of their investment in training when those workers' visas expired. Consequently, a number of firms committed to offering jobs to the refugees.

When we took the plan to the senior civil service, we received a mixed response that was at once enthusiastic and skeptical. On the one hand, they were excited by the proposal and were willing to back it enthusiastically. On the other hand, they let us know that all decision making was now centralized in the office of the prime minister and were skeptical about positive change forthcoming, even with business support. They estimated that such a proposal would take eighteen months to obtain approval. They helped us devise a more "diplomatic" proposal—specifically by deleting any specific reference to Syrian refugees which they believed would raise Harper's negatively oriented antennae. Further, they devised a method of including the idea under an existing program. In "the old days," this would have meant the program could be implemented within a few weeks. They let us know it would take four months at least. As it turned out, it was never implemented at all.

Despite the compatibility of the proposal with conservative business interests, the prime minister's office never supported the initiative. In October 2015, Justin Trudeau's Liberals defeated Stephen Harper's Conservatives with an unprecedented election plank to take in 25,000 Syrian refugees. This was a relatively low number given the enormous number of refugees in need of resettlement, but especially when compared to the government commitments to a much larger number of Indochinese refugees in 1979. However, it was unprecedented because it was the first time that a political party had made the intake of refugees a central part of its promised initiatives in running for election. In 1979–80, whenever questions arose about making refugee issues central to an election campaign, the idea was buried because, in an open debate, the anti-immigration sector of society would emerge and turn the proposal into a matter of great controversy.

The plan promised to bring the 25,000 refugees in by the end of the year. That was an extraordinary commitment which the experienced old hands resisted because logistically that was too large a number to bring in within such a short period. Further, given the way the staff in the immigration department had been reduced and for almost a decade had been denied any program initiatives on the administrative level, the department was seriously depleted. Most of the people with experience were gone and many of those who were left were unpracticed in taking responsibility and initiative. The task of taking in those refugees within two months would have been an enormous challenge for a civil service better prepared to tackle the problem, much less this one. The surprise, given these factors, was that the government, to its enormous credit, was able to deliver the program in a reasonable timeframe.

However, there were many problems. The forms that needed to be completed for private sponsorship were far more complicated than they were in 1979, and almost needed professional help to complete. Money for a year had to be shown up front rather than simply guaranteed. For speed, government-sponsored refugees were brought in first, which frustrated many refugee sponsors (as well as the privately sponsored refugees) and led to long waiting periods. Though the new program was widely supported by the media, that support lacked the enormous, sustained coverage that had been provided to the Indochinese refugee movement. Further, the private sector was riddled with many more tensions than had been the case in the 1980s, perhaps because organizations like Syria Lifeline lacked the organizing experience that the Indochinese sponsors had gained from being activists in the sixties.

The crisis was much worse, and Canada was in a far better position to bring in refugees, both because we had a far richer economy and were not immersed in a recession like the one in 1979. Besides, despite the weakened mandarin capacities, the government was determined to show it could deliver on its election promises. However, it lacked the experience to deliver on those promises, and it showed. Besides, the nature of giving seemed to have shifted. Humanitarians seemed to be much more oriented to more specific interests and ones closer to home. All these factors meant that the Syrian sponsorship movement and government support for Syrian refugees never reached the heights of the Indochinese refugee movement. The times had changed, and so had the ability to deliver on humanitarian obligations.

Sponsoring a Syrian Refugee Family

KATHARINE LAKE BERZ and JULIA HOLLAND

Our friendship began fifteen years ago when our sons were toddlers at the local preschool. We shared concerns about how to raise our children. How could we help them learn to read quickly? Should they play hockey or soccer? Should we worry that they were wearing their Halloween costumes to school in February? But above all, we worried about how to help our children become caring people. Most children in our Rosedale–Moore Park neighbourhood of Toronto enjoyed every possible material and educational advantage. Our children were studying in enriched and French immersion programs, learning piano from a venerated teacher, and participating in a multitude of sports and arts activities. How would they learn gratitude, generosity, and humility? There was no class for that.

We resolved to teach our children by example. Over the years, we collaborated with friends to contribute to our community in small ways. We raised funds for a Toronto urban hospital, supported orphaned youth in Ontario, and financed a program for AIDS victims in Swaziland. In the summer of 2015, the news of millions of displaced Syrians distressed us profoundly. We wanted to do more than contribute financially. We wanted to work together with our children to extend a personal welcome to as many Syrians as we could.

It took only a few weeks to gather a group of seven families who wanted to work together to sponsor one or two Syrian families. Our group included lawyers, finance professionals, management consultants, stay-at-home parents, a banker, a doctor, a nurse, and an accountant who were willing to share the varied tasks of settling a new family. When pictures emerged in the media of three-year-old Syrian Alan Kurdi lying dead on a Turkish beach, we had many more people wanting to join us. We contacted our local church, which had experience sponsoring refugees, and together we identified the best process to apply as sponsors. In a few months, seventeen other local sponsor groups formed to submit private applications in partnership with Rosedale United Church.

Then began a long wait for our family to arrive. Hundreds of other sponsorship groups had also formed in response to the newly elected government's commitment to resettle 25,000 Syrians, and we had to queue to be matched with an eligible family. Once offered a match, we had twenty-four hours to decide whether to accept the family based on the scant details of ages and health issues that were provided to us.

Our first match was a single mother with seven children. We were thrilled that our journey was about to begin. But two days later, we learned that the matching centre had mistakenly matched the family to two sponsorship groups, and we would not be sponsoring them after all. Days later, we were offered another family of seven. They had been farmers in Syria and had asked to be settled in a rural area. We were torn: was it fair to bring them to downtown Toronto? We shared our reservations with the matching centre and encouraged them to find a sponsorship group in a rural area, confident that they would, but noting that we would happily support the family if they did not. The centre found a rural match within the day.

Finally, in early February 2016, we were paired with a family who had four teenaged boys similar in ages to our own children. This felt like the right match for us. We researched neighbourhoods that would meet the family's needs, visited schools, and began gathering furniture and clothing. We waited for weeks, then months. Were they ill and unable to travel? Had they decided against coming to Canada? As we waited, the government was bringing Syrians to Canada by the planeload. Most were government-sponsored refugees who spent weeks in hotels before accommodations could be secured. In January 2016, there were 950 government-sponsored refugees living in hotels in the Toronto area. Affordable rentals in Toronto were becoming scarce, but we had secured a three-bedroom apartment for our family, not having any idea when they might arrive. We were outraged that so many refugees were living in limbo in hotels while hundreds of private groups like ours were waiting to help.

At the end of February 2016, the government hit its 25,000-refugee target and suddenly Syrians stopped arriving. The non-profit group, Canada for Refugees, reported that some 2,900 refugees who had been approved were still waiting to get on a plane to Canada, while hundreds of private groups in Canada were also waiting for a family to arrive, including us. The apartment we had rented was sitting furnished and empty. We joined meetings and protests to condemn the government's decision to slow down the processing of Syrian refugees. As the *Toronto Star* reported, on March 30, 2016, Arif Virani, then parliamentary secretary for Immigration Minister John McCallum, was faced with "an angry mob of do-gooders" at a public meeting organized by former Toronto mayor John Sewell. The next day, Minister McCallum announced that his staff would accept another 10,000 privately sponsored refugees.

Still, our family did not arrive, and so we started contacting our local MP, Chrystia Freeland, and other personal contacts in Ottawa to get more information. We learned that the mother of our matched family was pregnant and that they had not been cleared for travel. After numerous inquiries, we obtained a cellphone number for our family. We debated whether to call them. What could we say? In the end we decided against reaching out. It had the potential to be too upsetting for both sides, particularly given the information vacuum in which we operated, our inability to speak Arabic, and our powerlessness to influence the process.

By June 2016, our apartment had been sitting empty for four months and we decided to loan it to another refugee family. This family had been staying with a relative who was ill with cancer and needed new accommodations. They were highly educated Armenian Syrians from Aleppo, but had been living in a refugee camp in Jordan and arrived disheartened and overwhelmed. They had lived a good life in Syria and, to our surprise, longed for the stable days of the pre-Arab Spring authoritarian regime despite its abhorrent human rights record.

In early August, we were notified that the father of "our" family had been denied security clearance. Their case would be reviewed again, but we had no indication of their chances for eventual approval. We speculated on what the security issue might be. The father had been a member of the police force. They had four teenaged boys. The mother's fifth pregnancy ten years after her last seemed unusual, and we had heard that many refugees became pregnant hoping this would accelerate their cases. Our concerns grew.

We were faced with a difficult choice: Do we wait for this family, or do we ask to be matched with another family? How could we abandon them when the boys would so benefit from schooling in Canada? How could we deny this new baby a chance for a start in Canada? But what if the vetting process went on indefinitely? How many other homeless families might be on the list, hoping for good news?

In the end, we decided not to wait any longer, and within days we were matched with the Hassans (pseudonym), a couple with three small children and their grandmother. On October 6, 2016, we received notification that the Hassan family would arrive twelve days later. The Armenian family moved out of the apartment into Julia's house, and we began frantic last-minute preparations—school pre-registrations, immunization appointments, banking plans, clean linens, cellphones, household supplies, and groceries in the fridge. We put the finishing touches on a thick welcome binder, loaded with information, maps, and instructions in Arabic on everything that they could ever want to know about living in Toronto.

The Hassan family arrived at Pearson Airport, pushing all their belongings in one cart. We clutched a welcome sign in Arabic, not realizing at the time that the family was not able to read. We asked permission to shake hands. The Hassans were grateful to be off the plane. A translator provided the basic information—that for one year our group would provide financial and practical support. Mustafa, the father, was afraid of flying and had not slept for two nights. The children, aged eight, six, and one, were suffering from nausea and needed to change their clothes. Elham, a mother of three, was no more than twenty-five years old. Translated, her first words to us were: "Elham would like to go to school."

It would take many months for us to learn the Hassan family's story. But little by little, as they learned English, we learned more about them. They were Kurdish and had fled northern Syria on foot for Turkey four years prior. They had lived in a crowded apartment in Istanbul, hiding the children inside out of fear for their safety. Mustafa had worked intermittently and illegally as a labourer (painting, doing stucco, carrying heavy stones) and hotel cleaner for little pay and had endured verbal and physical abuse because of his ethnicity. They had received no health care and had never been to a dentist. As Elham explained, "A Kurd could lie dying outside the door of a hospital in Turkey and would not be let in." Only Mustafa had ever been to school, and then only for a couple of years before his father died and he had to work on the family's olive farm to support his mother. Mustafa's mother, Fatma, was developmentally delayed, could not care for herself, and suffered health complications from obesity. The children had very little muscle mass, having rarely played outside.

We had been prepared for the prospect that our refugee family might not speak any English. But we had not expected to learn that they were illiterate (and innumerate) in any language. Learning English, just to read a sign or a menu, would be a monumental task. This family had no education, no money of their own, and very uncertain employment prospects. The carefully assembled welcome binder was useless. But Elham and Mustafa had huge smiles and blistering determination to make a life in Canada. We were instantly smitten. The couple was technologically savvy and taught us to use technology to communicate. We would write our English phrase in a cell phone; they would scan the English text; use an app to translate it into Arabic text; and then use another app to translate the Arabic text into spoken Arabic.

The challenges the Hassans would face as uneducated and illiterate newcomers would be different from those that confronted their educated fellow Syrians, but not necessarily greater. Many educated newcomers had experienced the profound disappointment of giving up successful careers and having to settle for work that they felt was beneath them. Professionals found that their qualifications were not recognized. University students had to first perfect their English and then start their studies over again—if they could afford to. Struggles with depression were common.

The Hassans saw opportunity everywhere and were enthusiastic and willing to try anything. Within a week, all six of them were attending school. Within six weeks, they had all been in a swimming pool and to a skating rink for the first time. Fatma, who had never held a pen before, was using crayons to make marks. The older children—Nuhat, and her brother, Hamza—learned to ride bikes, and both they and their young sister, baby Hevrin, went on swings for the first time. Elham and Mustafa were eager to communicate and learned to speak English quickly.

We were grateful that our sponsor group was large. The family had a plethora of administrative appointments with settlement workers and immigration interviews. They had to get identity cards, health cards, sign a lease, open a bank account, and register for school. And we shuttled them to seemingly endless health appointments. The entire family had to endure a painstaking series of health exams with translators. They also had to receive in a few weeks all the childhood vaccinations that Canadians normally receive over a number of years. They were given nutrition appointments, contraception counselling, eye exams, and hearing tests. Each family member had appointments to provide urine, blood, and stool samples. And then there would be an uncertain lab result and we would have to repeat the process. Little Hevrin screamed her way through three gruelling blood extractions until we said, "Enough!" Fatma endured four cardiac tests, three mammograms, several cognitive assessments, and an overnight sleep test at the hospital. One of us kept "forgetting" to book Fatma her required colonoscopy. We decided to delay dental visits until one of the children complained of tooth pain before beginning a series of complex dental appointments.

English classes were both a joy and a source of great stress for Elham, Mustafa, and Fatma. They would start in Level 1 and would need to pass Level 4 to be granted a Canadian passport. Luckily, they had a good sense of humour, and when they were told that their initial assessment suggested that they should be in Level 0, they laughed: "Level 0! We are so bad at English they have to make a special level for us!" Elham relished her opportunity to learn and practiced her new words at every opportunity. Mustafa was frustrated to be the only man in a class full of beginners and worked quickly to be promoted to a higher level. Still, it will be a struggle for them to pass their Level 4. But they are desperate to be granted citizenship and a Canadian passport so they can travel to see their extended family again.

The children, having never been in a classroom environment, also struggled. Hamza in particular found it hard to adapt to the structures that Canadian children consider second nature. Standing in a line, sitting in a circle, and asking to go to the bathroom were as new to the children as the letters and numbers they practiced. By contrast, Hevrin, the baby, who attended a free daycare while her parents attended English classes, was soon learning both English and Kurdish with ease. The stimulating daycare was an added incentive for Elham and Mustafa to continue with their English courses.

The Hassan family did not appear to endure some of the cultural shock that other Syrian families experience in Canada. Only Fatma wore a head covering, and Mustafa was more engaged in household tasks than most Canadian fathers. But the cultural attitudes and ethnic prejudices they had learned in Syria and Turkey were difficult to change. We tried early on to describe Canada's tolerance for different cultures and traditions. We explained that we had LGBTQ friends and that members of our group were of Arab and Jewish origin. But unlearning takes time. Elham would point at women wearing burkas and say, "Arab terrible." They discouraged Nuhat from befriending the only other Syrian girl at her school because she was Arab. They resisted connecting with other Kurdish people that we knew because they were Iraqi.

But within a year of living in Canada both Elham and Mustafa had friends and work colleagues from different cultures. Mustafa befriended a Turkish neighbour who would often pick up the children from school for them. Elham secured a job in a Middle Eastern grocery store, serving "customers from every country." Although she still could not read, she was valued for her fluency in Kurdish, Arabic, Turkish, and now English.

Many other Syrian sponsor groups had to extend their financial support beyond the twelve-month commitment, but the Hassans were eager to get jobs before our sponsorship was fully complete. We concluded our financial transfers to them with enough money in our account to start thinking about sponsoring another family. With only a little help from us, both Mustafa and Elham secured jobs with the first employers that they approached. Mustafa, never having driven a car before, passed his road test after just four in-car lessons. They became determined to save money to buy a house. Still, at the time of writing, they have a long way to go to be fully independent. They cannot read their mail or notes from the children's school and are dependent on us to negotiate rent reviews, employment contracts, and cellphone terms. Banks, ATMs, and credit cards are still new to them.

As sponsors, we have learned a lot as well. Most importantly, we have learned that refugees are not "lucky." How many times have people told the Hassans how lucky they are? Sure, they are lucky that they were not in their village when it went up in flames. They are lucky that only one of their nephews and a few of their neighbours are dead. They are lucky that they did not catch deadly parasites from the scant food and untreated water in Syria and Turkey. But the family lives in constant fear for the safety of their friends and relatives. Fatma fears that she will never see her mother or brother again. Elham desperately misses her mother and nine siblings who are scattered in different countries around the world. Mustafa, despite all his optimism, goes through periods of deep sadness. He once told us he sometimes felt that he would rather be starving in his village than living comfortably here in Canada.

The second lesson we have learned is that sponsorship is not parent-hood. The Hassans were entirely dependent on us for the first few months to help them shop, attend appointments, and communicate with the children's teachers. We doted on them, but we were also very bossy. When they skipped English class or missed an appointment, we would reprimand them. We checked in each weekend to make sure that the children were getting to the park. We wished the adults would be more involved in the children's schooling and were frustrated when the dozens of books we and others had given them remained hidden away in the back of a closet. We were incensed when they spent "our money" to buy two new cellphones at over $1,000 each. It took some time, but we eventually realized that newcomers need to make their own decisions, even if they are "bad" decisions.

We had a party with our whole sponsor group to celebrate the Hassans' first year in Canada. The children played soccer, Fatma opened her birth-day gifts, and the adults traded memories of the year we had shared. We mentioned to Mustafa that he must be missing his extended family very much. "Family?" he replied, "I love my family. I have a very big family here in Canada."

Finding Welcome off the Refugee Highway

SHELLEY CAMPAGNOLA

Hardly a day goes by when there isn't something in the news about migrants, refugees, and asylum seekers in numerous countries around the world—stories about borders opening and borders closing; deportations and offshore rescues; families that have been separated and children that have been detained; or governments rising and falling on promises to keep people out or let people in. Fear and accusations give rise to anti-"other" public marches that are countered by marches demanding justice and humane treatment for the vulnerable. Historically, of course, the world has witnessed other waves of mass migration, but never anything on this scale.

For some, migration is voluntary, and we call it immigration. For others, it is forced, and we call it displacement. When persons who have been forcibly displaced come to Canada, they do so either as refugees who have already been granted permission to resettle here, or as asylum seekers—that is, those still seeking safety and who will subsequently claim refugee status.

COMING TO CONSCIOUSNESS

Like most people born and raised in Canada, my early understanding of refugee migration was limited to what I had learned in high school history and geography classes or had heard through the news. In other words, I really didn't know that much, and the events I did know about were far removed from me in distance and time. I had heard the term "refugee," but I didn't comprehend it. I was just happy that my country, Canada, was letting some stay (Vietnamese), and wondered why we were rejecting others (Tamils). It wasn't until 2004, when I began travelling for various work assignments, that I began to learn more about the complexities of refugee migration. The more I travelled for work in subsequent roles, the more I realized that what I had assumed was far removed from my own experience did in fact affect me personally and was in fact not far removed at all from the Canadian narrative.

One such trip took me to Arusha, Tanzania, to meet with a colleague who was working with orphaned children and single mothers in that city. We were both part of an international network of workers who were training workers and educators and advocating for the rights and needs of children at risk. As part of my orientation to his work, he took me to the International Criminal Tribunal for Rwanda, located since 1995 in Arusha. We stood outside the building and talked about the challenges of gaining justice in the face of overwhelming oppression.

As I stood there thinking about the role of this court in the wake of the Rwandan genocide, I became aware of the movement of people along the street. There were hundreds going in different directions—a seemingly endless line of humanity as far as my eye could see. I asked my colleague where they were going. "Nowhere," he said. "There is nowhere for them to go. They are just moving so that they aren't standing still." They were wanderers, with no destination before them, and no compelling force behind them to press them onward.

On another day in Arusha, we took time to visit a museum that documented the slave trade. I was shown the shackles that were used to restrain people and the posts where they were whipped to determine their value. My colleague spoke in detail, taking me, step by step, through the process of the selling of human beings as slaves. His stories troubled me deeply and I realized I had come as close as I had ever been, or ever hoped to be, to the slave trade. While the slave trade in Arusha had long since ended officially, I was aware then, and I am reminded today, that human trafficking and the slave trade remain rampant throughout the world. Researchers estimate that, as of 2016, more than 40 million people lived in conditions of modern slavery.[1] Refugees are some of those most vulnerable to exploitation, as they enter regions unfamiliar to them in their pursuit of safety.

My thoughts also turn to a Heritage Minutes video that celebrated Canada's role in the Underground Railroad.[2] This was a network of people from the 1830s to the 1860s who helped upwards of forty thousand people fleeing slavery find safety in Canada through five key entry points: Lakeshore, Dresden, Windsor, and Chatham, all in Ontario, and Birchtown, in Nova Scotia. I wonder if some of them had begun their lives in Arusha.

Since then, I have been to other countries in Africa, South America, Central America, and Europe and Eastern Europe, and, of course, I have made many visits to the United States. Except for the last, none of these visits have been for vacations; they have all been related to my work throughout the years. My travels and my involvement in matters related to refugee migration have exposed me to human suffering, and have affected me deeply. I have sat amid skeletal remains, bullet holes, and blood stains. I have hugged and talked with women who have been raped as a weapon of war, infected with AIDS, and left impoverished and abandoned by family and community. I have played soccer with young girls rescued from the sex trade and I have had lunch with teens who bear the brunt of oppression, religious persecution, and stolen inheritances. I have listened to people sing and have wondered how they could do so when they live surrounded by corruption, with threats against their lives, and restraints on their movements by economic, social, and political systems well beyond their control. I have watched helplessly as people have been reduced to primal fear by false accusations and threats of detention. I have wept at the end of long dark days, realizing that for many, life this way is normal—they have never known it to be any other way.

In 2007, I came across a saying that was attributed to an Aboriginal rights group in Australia: "If you have come to help me you can go home again. But, if you see my struggles as a part of your own survival, then perhaps we can work together." It is a quotation I come back to often when, as executive director of the Mennonite Coalition for Refugee Support (MCRS), I now sit on what some might call the "receiving end" of refugee migration. The

---

1 "Forced Labor, Modern Slavery, and Human Trafficking," International Labour Organization, http://www.ilo.org/global/topics/forced-labour/lang--en/index.htm.

2 "Underground Railroad," 1991, Historica Canada, https://www.historicacanada.ca/content/heritage-minutes/underground-railroad.

MCRS (soon to be renamed the Compass Refugee Centre) is an organization that seeks to assist, accompany, and advocate for people who have made it to Canada to seek asylum for themselves and their families.

WELCOME TO CANADA?

A now famous tweet by Prime Minister Trudeau in late January 2017 was a catalyst for putting the asylum process in Canada on the stand for public cross-examination: "To those fleeing persecution, terror & war, Canadians will welcome you, regardless of your faith. Diversity is our strength #WelcomeToCanada." Trudeau's tweet was in sharp contrast to a recent policy shift in the United States that would see people from certain Muslim countries excluded from the asylum process there. The subsequent influx of people crossing into Canada from the US seemed to be directly related to that tweet. But to suggest that such a statement of welcome in the face of the unwelcoming approach to the south was the sole reason why people came to Canada is to fail to consider the historical trends, global realities, policies, public perception, and political navigation of a world that produces refugees.

Among the formal and informal policies that have affected the welcome, or lack thereof, for refugee claimants is the Safe Third Country Agreement (STCA) between Canada and the United States, which came into effect in 2004. A "safe third country" is defined as a country where an individual, on passing through that country, could have made a claim for refugee protection. The purpose of the agreement was to enable both governments to better manage access to their own refugee system in response to people crossing the shared border at land points. It applies only to refugee claimants, and it worked well for Canada at first, reducing the number of people coming through the United States and seeking refugee status in Canada.

When the policies and attitudes toward refugees and immigrants in the United States changed in 2017, it also brought into question how safe the United States was for refugees. Reports of undocumented people being detained and deported at shockwave speed spurred a negative ripple effect far beyond the shared border with Canada. People who might have tried to claim refugee status in the United States now wanted to steer clear of that country and come straight to Canada. Even those already in the process of claiming refugee status in the United States heard, and experienced, a clear message that they were not welcome, and began making their way north.

Because the agreement between the two countries is applied only at official border checkpoints, increasing numbers of people crossed, and, at the time of writing, continue to cross, the border between such points. Yes, this is an illegal act, but it is a way to counter what has been deemed an untenable policy that leaves those seeking refuge with no opportunity for a fair hearing. Justice Michael Phelan recognized as much in his November 2007 Federal Court decision that followed a legal challenge brought by several organizations, including the Canadian Council for Refugees. In his decision he wrote, "Several aspects of U.S. law put genuine refugees at risk of *refoulement* to persecution and/or *refoulement* to torture," and then he went on to argue:

> It is therefore quite clear that the life, liberty and security of refugees is put at risk when Canada returns them to the U.S. under the STCA if the U.S. is not in compliance with CAT [the Convention Against Torture] and the Refugee Convention. The law in the U.S. with respect to gender claims and the material support bar, along with the other issues found to be contrary to the Convention, make it "entirely foreseeable" that genuine claimants would be *refouled*. The situation is potentially even more egregious in respect of *refoulement* to torture. A refugee, by his/her very nature, is fleeing a threat to his/her life, liberty or security, and a risk of return to such conditions would surely engage section 7 [of the Canadian Charter of Rights and Freedoms]. There is sufficient causal connection between Canada and the deprivation of those rights by virtue of Canada's participation in the STCA.[3]

He further wrote that "there is evidence that people from countries which are powerless to stop torture or from countries where terrorist organizations routinely extort money will be disproportionately affected. It will be especially hard for these individuals to prove genuine refugee claims in the U.S. This is a burden which other claimants entering at the land border do not bear."[4]

Although the Federal Court of Appeal subsequently overturned the decision, it did so on technical grounds—that is, it did not rule that the United States *is* a country safe for all refugees. A new challenge to the Safe Third

---

3 *Canadian Council for Refugees v. R.*, 2007 FC 1262, https://www.canlii.org/en/ca/fct/doc/2007/2007fc1262/2007fc1262.html, at paras. 283 and 285.

4 Ibid., at para. 324.

Country Agreement was brought in July 2017, and in July 2020 the STCA was again struck down. Federal Court Justice Ann Marie McDonald found that the agreement violates the constitutional guarantee of life, liberty and security. As she wrote,

> Failed claimants are detained without regard to their circumstances, moral blameworthiness, or their actions. They are detained often without a release on bond and without a meaningful process for review of their detention. While responsibility sharing may be a worthwhile goal, this goal must be balanced against the impact it has on the lives of those who attempt to make refugee claims in Canada and are returned to the US in the name of "administrative efficiency" (*Bedford* at para 121). In my view, imprisonment cannot be justified for the sake of, and in the name of, administrative efficiency.[5]

At the time of this writing, that decision is being appealed by the Government of Canada.

Caught in the middle of all these legal challenges are the refugee claimants themselves, who risk deportation to the very danger they have fled if they cross at a border point and risk their well-being, even life, if they cross between border points. People who make it across the border must complete an initial application (in either English or French) and be interviewed by an officer of the Canada Border Services Agency (CBSA), who will decide whether they are eligible to remain in Canada to make a refugee claim. If so, they are handed what is currently called a "Confirmation of Referral" letter, an application package that includes a "Basis of Claim" form that must be submitted to the Immigration and Refugee Board (IRB) within fifteen days, and a list of organizations that might be able to help them. They are then sent off to find their own way. In 2017, a year after I joined the MCRS, 559 people found their way to the organization. Add to these people those who had come before them and those who have come since. That brings the number of people we are presently helping through the refugee claim process up to over 1,600 men, women, and children.

---

5 *Canadian Council for Refugees v. Canada (Immigration, Refugees and Citizenship)*, 2020 FC 770, https://www.canlii.org/en/ca/fct/doc/2020/2020fc770/2020fc770.html, at para. 135.

I am often asked about the financial situation of the asylum seekers and the money they used to get to Canada. Behind the question is the perception that refugees shouldn't be able to travel all the way to Canada and then claim they have nothing so that they can be dependent on social assistance. The question is magnified by media stories of people with nice suitcases, clean clothes and white teeth crossing the border, leaving cellphones dumped on the other side. It is disheartening to read what people write about these things on social media platforms. The images we have at MCRS are of real people who have experienced or seen many things. When we meet them, they sit across from us holding desperately onto the last shreds of personal dignity, hoping we believe them and that we can help them prepare to tell their story to the one person at the IRB who will decide if they can stay in Canada.

These people have names and hopes and dreams. They had full lives and were raising their families and caring for loved ones and celebrating the milestones in life we all celebrate. Some are former government officials who spoke out against rampant corruption. Some are human rights activists who lobbied against abuse and exploitation. Some are journalists who were imprisoned and tortured for daring to write the truth. Some are families who dared to pray that God would bring about change so that their children would be safe in their communities and not be dragged off to child labour or to be a child soldier. Some are businesspeople who said no to extortion in countries overrun by gangs. Some are women who have escaped human trafficking. Some are fathers whose families were killed because of their refusal to engage in drug smuggling. Some are couples whose children were kidnapped as a warning to stay silent about the crimes they witnessed. Some are mothers who are trying to keep their daughters from being mutilated. Some are brothers who bravely agreed to testify against organized crime. Some are children whose parents were murdered for trying to do the right thing. Some are sons and daughters whose pictures are in the local newspaper so that they can be hunted down and killed for their sexual orientation. We have even worked with people who have been tracked around the world by the people who were targeting them.

When refugees arrive, many of them only have the clothes on their back and a few small personal items, including pictures of family members they had to leave behind. When they fled their countries of origin, they could only afford to get one person out of danger. They hope, now they are here, that they can work on getting their families to safety as well. Little do they know that many of them will not be reunited for years. The wait will be long enough that their families will start to believe they are not wanted. In the worst situations, their families will not survive. Families of refugees have been found in their places of hiding and killed or have died trying to cross dangerous terrain, hoping to speed up their own safety or family reunification.

Refugees need shelter, they need food to eat, they need warm clothes, and they need a good long sleep. Except that many of them can't sleep, at least not all that well. They have been through much, they are desperately missing their families, and they don't have assurance that they won't be sent back. The food is different, the temperature is cold, and very few of the people around them, if any, speak their language. They don't like being on social assistance. For most of them, there was no such thing in their home country, but here they have no choice until they are granted a work permit and can find employment. It's even harder when they begin to understand that they are perceived by so many to be "tax-takers" and "frauds" for having received the help offered. It is even harder still when the money refugees do receive isn't enough to pay the bills, which means they must go to food and clothing banks to make ends meet.[6]

They also need help filling out the numerous forms that they are required to submit, which are daunting even for someone already fluent in English or French. I wonder how many of us could do this without help or supporting documents in front of us, even if we hadn't also gone through the traumatic experiences and upheaval claimants go through. They must also answer the all-important question—the basis of their claim—in which they have to provide details of the harm they experienced, including dates, times, other people involved, and reasons why they think it happened. Each family member's claim is considered separately. If parents have children under six, they must explain why those children should not be returned to their country

---

6 At the time of writing, a single person with no children in Ontario is given $733 per month; a couple with two children under eighteen will receive $1,250 a month ("Ontario Works Rate Chart, October 1, 2018," https://www.toronto.ca/wp-content/uploads/2017/11/99bb-ontario-works-rate-chart-oct2017-tess.pdf). This is supposed to cover basic needs and shelter. Even in Ontario's smaller cities, it is all but impossible to rent a one-bedroom unit for under $1,000. In downtown Toronto, at the time of writing, the average monthly rent for a one-bedroom apartment is now well over $2,000.

separate from any harm that could come to them as a parent. We have seen children be accepted but not their parents, and vice versa. We have seen only one parent and some or none of the children accepted. We have seen grandparents who are dependent on their children deported.

They have fifteen days to get their refugee claim in. That includes weekends but not statutory holidays. That gives us fifteen days (if they get to us on the first day) to help them get the documents completed and translated, acquire legal aid and a lawyer, and then get it all submitted. What ends up on those documents will determine the rest of their lives. The Canadian public demanded quick processing, and that's what the government gave them. The fact that, after that, hearings are often delayed because of a lack of government resources is another matter. As of January 2020, the IRB was estimating that refugee claimants would wait an average of 22 months for a hearing.[7] In the meantime, they must gather the evidence that supports their claim. Police reports, eyewitness statements, newspaper clippings (all of which must be translated), pictures of scars on their body showing the torture or other harm they experienced, and any other official reports that could corroborate their story must be pulled together and submitted to the IRB no later than ten days before the date of their hearing.

If they came from one of the top five countries we see represented in our office (Colombia, Turkey, Eritrea, Iran, and Venezuela), getting that information is not easy. The closest country is almost 6,392 kilometres away, and the furthest is almost 12,000 kilometres away. Most of us do not carry around the kind of information that is needed for the application, and if you have bullets whizzing past your head, you aren't thinking about grabbing evidence. A year, two years, or ten years down the road, refugee claimants in Canada will have their final answer. If they are lucky, they will go to the airport and welcome family members who are at long last able to join them in their new, safe home. If they are not, they will have been deported back to the dangers they fled.

While we are not able to track everyone who is deported, we have been able to track enough of them to know that some do not live much longer after arriving back in their home country. Some are murdered—their fears,

7 "Making a Claim for Refugee Protection? Here's What You Should Know," Immigration and Refugee Board of Canada, last modified January 22, 2020, https://irb-cisr.gc.ca/en/information-sheets/Pages/refugee-protection.aspx.

which were not believed in Canada, now fulfilled. Others go into hiding or try to flee to yet another country. Still others manage to survive, but often in unimaginably cruel situations. Sometimes deportation divides families, depriving children of their father or mother simply because the two were originally from different countries. Rules are rules, and each parent is sent back to his or her country of citizenship, even if legally married, no matter the senselessness of the decision.

OUTCOMES

What has been highlighted in this chapter are personal observations, and some of the key policies and public perceptions that affect refugee claimants. The world is in upheaval. People are on the move. Some of those people—refugee claimants—have a personal target on their back. They travel thousands of kilometres through all kinds of peril, many of them separated from their families and everything they have known. They go from country to country trying to be heard and trying to find refuge. Instead, they find closed borders, anti-refugee sentiment, and too often, laws and policies meant to deter people from coming rather than being intended to welcome them, listen to them, and provide them the protection they need.

The asylum system itself is a complex one that mixes politics, policies of scrutiny and suspicion, public perceptions, and opinionated rhetoric with the personal pain of real people. It tries to bring justice while not upsetting local budgets, international relationships, economic trading partners, and voters who too often are ill-informed and easily inflamed by incomplete media reporting.

It is also a system that is built to make fast decisions but was not given the "gas"—the people resources—to do so. Thus it leaves people waiting years to hear if they are safe at last and can bring their families to be with them. And it leaves the public thinking the system doesn't work.

At MCRS, we have helped thousands of people since we first began in 1987. Without help from organizations like ours, we estimate that more than half of those people would have been sent back to the very things they were seeking protection from. They wouldn't have understood the process or the documents well enough to be successful. They wouldn't have kept up with the ever-changing policies or have met the tight deadlines. They wouldn't have had help settling in the community and rebuilding their lives with new sights, sounds, tastes, weather, and so much more. They wouldn't have had someone advocating for them when they were being misrepresented in the public domain. They wouldn't have had someone lobbying for changes to policies that jeopardized their well-being. They wouldn't have had someone crying with them when they learned a family member (or two or three) died while waiting to come.

Given the state of the world, we can be certain that refugee claimants will keep coming until a day arrives when our country closes its borders too. Given how perceptions can change from one season to the next, we will either welcome people openly or we will make it difficult, hoping to deter others. May there be enough of us who believe that the human story should be heard, and that people's dignity should be protected and restored when others have taken it away. May there be enough of us to ensure that the opportunity to be *safe at last* may be realized by those who have no place else to go.

My Experience as a Refugee and Settlement Worker

EUSEBIO GARCIA

In November 1984, my brother Luis Enrique and I fled the civil war in El Salvador and headed for Texas where another one of my brothers, Abelino, had been living and working for some years as a non-status person. All three of us were arrested, put in detention, and separated while crossing the Mexico/United States border. I was only nineteen at the time, spoke no English, and felt very nervous about what might happen to me. I did not understand the detention review process and why that system was re-traumatizing me. Fortunately, the other detainees, as well as a lawyer from a place called "Proyecto Libertad" who visited me periodically, were reassuring, telling me everything would be okay and that eventually I would be released and reunited with my older brothers. Their presence helped me through a very anxious time. After three months, my bond amount (a cash deposit, like bail) was decreased and Abelino, who had already been released, was able to pay it. Although my brothers and I were freed from detention, we were still without status and our future was uncertain.

Our original plan was to travel to Canada where another brother, José Agustin, had been living for a year. He filled me in on what was happening at Friends House, which was the home of the Society of Friends (Quakers) in Toronto. Friends House was *the* place for Central American refugees to assemble and organize in the 1980s. Every Thursday, refugees from Central America would gather there to talk about the war, and to plan actions such as demonstrations in front of the United States consulate, protesting American aid to repressive Central American governments. Nancy Pocock, Fred Franklin, Isabelle Showler, and Erika Whitney were some of the incredible Quakers who were there for us. While Spanish was our language of communication, there was always someone there to translate into English. José told Nancy about our predicament in Texas, and she got the ball rolling on our resettlement in Canada. We arrived in Toronto on December 13, 1985, and were taken from the airport to Hotel Isabella, downtown. What I remember most from this time was how *cold* it was! I didn't want to leave the building as I hoped for the weather to get better before going outside. After two weeks in Canada, I went to a Thursday meeting at Friends House and got involved with the Central American refugee community. I took English classes at George Brown College and later studied social work there. The course combined in-class learning with work experience, and in my first year I took a work placement at Friends House to help newcomers to Canada find jobs. I soon discovered what a rewarding experience this was. Although the jobs were usually entry-level positions, the newcomers were happy to gain Canadian experience, and I felt great being able to help.

In my second year at George Brown, I took a placement in Family Benefits (now known as the Ontario Disability Support Program), where I encountered many mental health issues among my clients. Although I had worked with people facing hardships before, this was on a different scale, and the experience wore me down. When a full-time position as a refugee settlement worker came up at Friends House in October 1990, I eagerly applied and got the job. I started working with Nancy Pocock, an amazing woman who tirelessly advocated for refugees. Nancy founded the Toronto Monthly Meetings of the Quaker Committee for Refugees.

DIRECT SERVICE PROGRAM AT FRIENDS HOUSE (QUAKER HOUSE)

The needs of displaced persons and refugees has long been part of Friends' work in Toronto through the work and support of former and present Quaker Committee for Refugees members, the Toronto Monthly Meeting, and Quaker foundations. The committee has gone from assisting Central Americans to serving people from all parts of the world. Our specific aim is to provide assistance to refugees both during and after the application process in the areas of translation and interpretation, application to social services, finding shelter on arrival, obtaining legal aid services, inland and overseas family sponsorship applications, detention-related matters, medical and school appointments, and other settlement services. In addition, our committee members spend a lot of their time speaking to local and national politicians and creating awareness of refugee issues within the Quaker community and the community at large. We also offer follow-up support with family reunification and citizenship applications.

Our committee holds two big events every year. For Labour Day weekend, I bring a group of immigrants and refugees up to Camp NeeKauNis, a Quaker summer camp located in Waubanshene, a beautiful town 160 kilometres north of Toronto. Here they can experience nature, canoeing, swimming, and playing soccer. They also participate in an art program and a musical evening at the camp. This not only gives newcomers a taste of Canada's beauty, but also strengthens bonds between different families so they can support each other. I also organize a Christmas party for refugees at Friends House, a celebration attended every year by over a hundred children and their parents. The event has been ongoing for more than twenty-five years and is a wonderful way to make a difference for newcomers during the holiday season. It is a chance for kids to sing and play classic carols, meet "the man in red," share stories, eat great food and leave with a gift to be unwrapped on Christmas Eve.

IMMIGRATION HOLDING CENTRE IN TORONTO

Many years after my departure from my homeland, I find myself interviewing detainees at the Immigration Holding Centre in Toronto to find out their needs and offer orientation and assistance. Where appropriate, I refer them to the Refugee Law Office for representation at detention reviews, to legal aid, or to the Toronto Bail Program when release appears achievable. The detention population includes persons attempting to make refugee claims, those awaiting a decision on their claim, and those who have had their refugee claims refused. Also at the Centre are persons attempting to enter Canada as visitors, persons who have lived in Canada without status, and those who have overstayed their visas. The population at the Centre includes women and men who come from all over the world. Until recently, children were also detained.

The detention environment is hard on all those involved. Those with valid passports can be deported very swiftly, leaving their families, businesses, and possessions in Canada. It is particularly upsetting when parents are being deported with their Canadian children, or with a child who has a serious medical problem. Others frequently need support in helping adjust to the reality of being forced to return home. Here are a couple of stories that I have been personally involved with at the Immigration Holding Centre.

A Failed Refugee Claimant

Josefa (not her real name) came to Canada when she was seven months pregnant. The father of her child joined her four months after her arrival. A consultant made errors related to their cases that resulted in Josefa's partner ending up in detention for a year before he was deported to Nigeria. Her partner was killed a few months after being removed from Canada. Josefa remained in Canada with her refugee claim still open until eventually her application was also rejected. When she refused to leave Canada voluntarily, she was detained, along with her daughter, who was now six years old. Prior to Josefa's detention, her lawyer had applied on her behalf for admission to Canada on the basis of humanitarian and compassionate considerations, which was accepted only when our office managed to gather evidence that her partner had been killed in Nigeria. This time she received a positive decision on her application, after having been detained with her daughter for more than six months at the Immigration Holding Centre. Josefa is now fully employed, and she and her daughter are finally settling in Canada.

Crossing from the United States

Miguel (not his real name) had worked for many years in the United States as a subcontractor for a flooring company—he had no status in the US. The company sent him to do a project in Liverpool, New York, which consisted of installing a ceramic floor at a sports bar. Miguel and some other men arrived in New York on July 17, 2017. The job took them about three weeks to finish.

Before heading back to Texas, the majority of the men that Miguel had travelled with wanted to take advantage of the fact that they were near Niagara Falls and wanted to go and see them because they all knew that it was unlikely that they would be back in this part of the country anytime soon. The driver of the vehicle, a friend who also had no status in the United

States, got confused following the signs on the highway, and they ended up in the line waiting to cross into Canada and by the time they realized what had happened, they had passed the point where they could turn around. Since Miguel was an undocumented worker in the United States, he knew this spelled trouble. When their turn came, the officer at the border asked them to provide their identification. They all had some form of identification from Mexico, but no passports. Because they could not provide legitimate identification, they were informed that they had two options: they could return to the United States, or they had the right to make a claim for refugee protection in Canada. Miguel decided to claim refugee status. The car was seized by Canadian authorities and Miguel was detained and sent to the Immigration Holding Centre in Toronto, where I had the opportunity to hear part of his refugee claim story.

Miguel decided to submit his application as he was certain that, if he returned to the United States, he would be quickly deported to Mexico. He couldn't understand why he had been detained and he asked to see a bond person to be able to get out of the holding centre. He began by telling me that his life was in danger in Mexico because he would be targeted by members of organized criminal gangs like the Zetas that are present in almost every single state of Mexico. It is well known that illegal immigrants that are deported back to Mexico face far greater risk than the average citizen because of the misconception that they have money. It does not matter how hard you try to explain to these criminals that you have just been deported and have no money, no assets, and very often no family and no place to sleep. They do not care about your problems, and choose instead to harass their victims, kidnap them, beat them, torture, and sometimes kill them. Their family members, including parents, siblings, cousins, spouses, and children are often kidnapped as well and only released upon receipt of the requested ransom.

Miguel knew about some friends of his cousins that returned to Mexico of their own accord about a year before. They went missing and their family members in Mexico believed they had been murdered. About three years ago, two of his ex-wife's cousins, whom he always knew as "El topo" and "La eléctrica," returned to Mexico. Shortly after their return they went missing. Their father saw strangers driving their car and notified the authorities. About a month after their disappearance he was given the dismembered bodies of his two children by the authorities. Miguel knew that the Zetas had murdered many vulnerable migrants in the past and have buried their bodies in shallow graves.

He feared returning to Mexico because he knew he would be exposed to a higher risk of violence after having lived in the United States. He was certain that he would be harassed, targeted, attacked, and very possibly murdered because these criminals believed that they and their families had money saved up and they would try to get money from them through extortion and kidnapping. Miguel believed that if he were returned to Mexico, he would meet this same fate. For these reasons, he asked the Canadian government to consider his application for refugee protection in Canada. If given the opportunity, he would embrace the chance to become a hard-working, useful member of the Canadian society.

An Unaccompanied Minor at the Immigration Holding Centre

I helped Ahmed (not his real name), a very talkative teenager from Syria, get legal representation to be allowed to stay in Canada. First, I discovered that he had tried to make a refugee claim at the Fort Erie border as an unaccompanied minor, which resulted in his being placed in isolation at the Immigration Holding Centre. It was shocking to me to see a kid from Syria, the very country from which Canada has decided to take 25,000 refugees for resettlement, being ordered deported, and not being allowed to contact his family or to socialize with the rest of the detainee population. There was no reason to detain him as he was not considered to be a danger to the public. Furthermore, detaining children is supposed to be a last resort. Now here he was, sitting across the table from me and trying to understand what was happening to him. He began by telling me that he was living in Egypt with his family when his residency permit expired. He faced being sent back to Syria, where he would most likely be recruited into the Army. Fearing the worst, his parents decided that the best place for him was Canada. Ahmed had already suffered war in his country and had fled under dangerous conditions to another country. Now he had to face the threat of being deported back to his war-torn country. Finally, he was sent to Canada on his own, where he ended up in solitary confinement. It was during this time of re-traumatization that he had to justify that he was a refugee and plead for protection.

I connected Ahmed with a lawyer who helped him get started with an immigration process that not only delayed his deportation, but ended up getting him released from the holding centre after being granted first-stage approval for permanent residence on humanitarian and compassionate grounds by Minister of Immigration John McCallum.

These stories are three of many real-life tragedies for people who are considered low-risk detainees, but who lack immigration status in Canada. There are many other human beings who face long periods of detention and having to deal with ID issues and detention reviews, refugee hearings, and interviews all the time. It is for this reason that detention has always been at the heart of the work of the Quaker Committee for Refugees in Toronto. For those individuals making a refugee claim, the Immigration and Refugee Board's written decision is a foundational document to start living a normal life in Canada. It is critical for them to envision a future in their new country. On the day they receive IRB approval, they can start dreaming of the time when they will be reunited with their loved ones who are still overseas. Locally, many of them find it hard to focus on work, study, and integration until they know that they have been allowed to live here permanently.

The Friends don't work alone; we are also part of national and provincial networks such as the Canadian Council for Refugees and the Ontario Coalition of Agencies Serving Immigrants. We all dream of a fair immigration and refugee protection system under which refugees and immigrants can feel more secure and welcome. I hope the above stories can help Canadians learn about the realities many human beings face every single day as they try to get permanent resident status in this country.

part three

THE STRUGGLE FOR
INCLUSION

From Chilean Refugee to Canadian Citizen

PABLO POLICZER

with an illustrated account by

ADAM POLICZER *and* IRENE POLICZER

Santiago, Chile, September 11, 1973. It was a Tuesday, and I was eight years old. I listened to the radio that morning in the living room with my sisters and Elena, our nanny. My parents kept us home from school, but they went to work. Or at least they tried to go to work. Dad worked a few blocks from La Moneda, the presidential palace. He heard the bombs fall and smelled the smoke. Mom worked across the street from La Moneda and saw and felt the bombing up close. Each decided to return home instead of staying to put up a futile resistance.

The Chilean armed forces overthrew President Salvador Allende's government on the morning of September 11, 1973. We heard Allende's last broadcast over the radio: "The Air Force has bombed . . . history is ours . . ." I didn't completely understand what was happening, but my parents supported the Allende government and the Socialist revolution it was trying to bring about, and I knew this was serious.

Elena couldn't hide her own fear, especially because for several hours we didn't know where my parents were or whether they would make it home.

Dad returned first, and then mom several hours later. It would take years for me to understand the consequence for all of us of the decisions they'd made that day. People around them had stashed some weapons in anticipation of the coup, and many decided to use them. Dad, especially, considered joining them, but in the end, he came home. Many of those who held out were killed, many more imprisoned. Years later, I learned that those early days were the deadliest. Many people were brutally tortured and killed with impunity. Had my parents stayed put, our lives would have been different.

Instead dad was arrested a couple of months later, in early December. He had a car—a Citroën 2CV, or "Citroneta"—and drove a friend to the French embassy. The plan was to help him hop the fence to seek asylum. They drove by the embassy and saw that it was guarded by soldiers. They drove by a second time, but no luck. They paused for a smoke and coffee and decided to try one last time. They were stopped. The friend was kicked out of the country a week later, and my father was kept as a political prisoner.

We didn't know where he was at first, and I remember the tension at home. Mom, my grandparents, all the adults. No one knew, and no one told us. This was an adult problem, and children were kept in the dark. But some kids did know. My friend Daniel, who was a little older than me and whose own father had gone into hiding, teased me about it. Didn't I know that my dad was in prison? I forced mom to tell me, and she brought me into the secret. She didn't know much at first, but suspected dad had been taken prisoner. She asked me not to tell my younger sisters, Ana and Catalina, who were six and four at the time. I was still a child, but as the oldest, being entrusted with this heavy secret was a step into the burdens of adulthood. The idea was to protect my sisters by not telling them. Later, as teenagers, each of them would express how bewildering it had been to be kept in the dark about the real reason for dad's absence.

We began to get some concrete information after about a week. He'd been held by the civilian police force, and then transferred to a detention centre run by the Army in the Estadio Chile, the covered basketball arena downtown. At least he was alive. It must have been weeks later when mom and I went to visit him. He appeared from behind the barriers inside the stadium, walking toward us in a trench coat. I cried with relief, finally seeing him in the flesh.

Again, years later when researching this period, I would learn that dad was fortunate. He wasn't captured during the brutal chaos in September just after the coup, but also not during early 1974, when a deadly new secret police force would begin to simply make people disappear. Despite disappearing for about a week, he was instead processed in a more bureaucratic way. His name appeared on lists of prisoners. The International Committee of the Red Cross knew where he was, and so did we. It was harder for the regime to kill people others were watching. If he'd been detained a couple of months later, he would most likely have disappeared without a trace.

He spent a year and a half as a political prisoner. First six months in the Estadio Chile, then six months up north in Chacabuco, an abandoned desert mining town converted to a concentration camp, then back near Santiago by the coast for about a month, then under house arrest until he was finally released in June 1975. During this time, mom kept her job as an urban planner in the Ministry of Public Works, now working directly under the military officers in charge. They knew that her husband was in prison, that she was trying to get him released, and that she wanted to leave the country. Trained as an architect, like dad, she also worked overtime to look after his clients while he was in prison. Years later, I would also learn how hard it was for her with the heavy burden of caring for three children and keeping up dad's practice, while being forced to work for the regime that kept her husband in prison.

My school also changed after the coup. It was a public school with a reputation for being progressive, but one day soldiers appeared and took over. Long hair was forbidden, and we had to line up and sing the national anthem in front of the flag every morning. Years later I would learn that some of my teachers were expelled, but at the time I still went to class and played soccer with my friends at recess. The teachers who remained tried to keep things as normal as possible, as did the adults in my family, with birthday parties, Christmas presents, and trips to the seaside. But there was tension and fear. I knew I had to be careful about what I said and to whom. I knew about prisoners and feared I might be detained as well. At home we talked about what to do if soldiers came looking for something or someone. The golden rule was not to say anything. One of the books my parents got rid of shortly after the coup, along with the obviously political ones, was a textbook on reinforced concrete—*El hormigón armado*. They feared soldiers might misinterpret the title, as *armado* can also mean "armoured" or "armed."

I hid under the covers of my parents' bed, pretending that soldiers were walking by, and practising being perfectly still so they wouldn't find me.

I rode on the back of a friend's Citroneta, lying on the flat bed, with eyes closed, pretending to be a blindfolded prisoner. Ana and I played a game to figure out only from the movement of the car where they were taking us. When dad was in prison, I regularly woke up in fear, screaming in the middle of the night, convinced that intruders had entered the house. I forced mom to get out of bed to help me look for them. Without dad around, I felt responsible for keeping our home safe.

The adults talked about places like England, France, Australia, Venezuela, and Canada. Mom took us to the Canadian embassy at one point. We knew people who'd emigrated there. The visa to Canada was issued just after dad's release. We later suspected that an officer in the ministry might have helped mom by facilitating dad's release, in anticipation of a visa that would take us out of the country. But we don't know.

The original plan was for all five of us to leave in June, after dad was free and as soon as the visa was issued. But I contracted typhoid fever, and then gave it to Ana. No entry to Canada for sick children. Perhaps no entry for any of us. It took some pleading for Canada to allow dad to travel first, and for the rest of us to follow. At that time Chilean refugees could still choose where to land. My parents consulted their encyclopedia, and saw that Vancouver had the mildest climate. The decision to move to Vancouver—one of the most consequential my family ever took—was based on nothing more complicated than fear of the cold.

We spent about three months apart. My first images of Canada came from a picture book: mountains, forests, snow, and moose. Dad's letters added new elements: Vancouver had a beautiful downtown park, and there were squirrels and crows. I couldn't wait to see this new land with exotic animals. Mom, Ana, Catalina, and I left Santiago on September 18, 1975, which was Chilean Independence Day. On the way to the airport we drove past flags and celebrations everywhere. Also soldiers on the street and helicopters overhead. Our dog, Tino, ran after us for many blocks. We learned later that he returned only after several days, emaciated, and died not long after. A part of us also died with him, I think. As the plane rose into the air, I felt relief.

We landed in Vancouver the next morning. Mountains, water, trees, all clean, fresh, modern. Together again, in a new home. One of the first things my parents did was to put me and my sisters in front of the television to watch *Sesame Street*. "You have to learn English," they told us. Dad spoke from experience. He's Jewish, born in Hungary in 1938. He lost his mother and most of his family in the camps during the War and arrived as a seven-year old refugee in Chile in 1946. We were both about the same age when we became refugees, and he knew that the way to survive was to adapt, to integrate. He had become Chilean as a child, and now our task was to become Canadian.

We started school soon after arriving with Ana and Catalina in regular classes and me in an ESL program. There were kids from different parts of the world. I'd never met anyone from India, China, Iran, Germany, or Sweden. We sang songs and played games. I slept well now, with only bits of English intruding into my dreams. In Santiago, once we knew we were going to Canada and would have to learn English, I had trouble imagining what that would be like. Canadians must translate into Spanish, I told my friends, because how could anyone think in any language other than Spanish? Impossible. But about a month after starting school, I caught myself in the playground, thinking in English for the first time. It was easy after that. I still had a lot to learn, but thinking in English without translating made all the difference.

Years later, I came to understand that we were lucky to have landed in Vancouver just as Canada was embracing a new politics of multiculturalism. In recent years there has been more resistance to the arrival of immigrants and refugees, but at the time the message we heard everywhere was "Welcome, you're a new Canadian." Yes, we were different, but so was everyone else in a society that embraced those differences. Chileans stuck together, forming associations and organizations to raise money for the resistance against the dictatorship, but we didn't live apart, in a ghetto. We struggled financially, as my parents worked hard to validate their credentials, study, and find work. But we integrated in school, and after a while my parents landed on their feet. Mom worked in her field as an urban planner and dad in his as an architect. Canada embraced us as we became Canadian.

The community of Chileans in Vancouver was small but tightly knit, even while it reproduced many of the political and class divisions in Chile. A key question was "When did you arrive?" Most Chileans landed after the coup, beginning in early 1974. But a few, wealthier and more conservative, had arrived in 1970, fleeing the newly elected Marxist government. They took their capital out of the country when it elected a government intent on taking over the means of production. I became friends at school with kids from those families. And even among the larger community of refugees from the dictatorship, there were divisions. Years later, as a political scientist, I learned that Chile has one of the strongest party systems in Latin America. As a teenager in Vancouver, I experienced the way Chileans sorted themselves out along party lines, especially Communists versus members of the Movement of the Revolutionary Left (Movimiento de Izquierda Revolucionaria, or MIR). Dad had been a member of Salvador Allende's Socialist Party, and I went to some Socialist events early on, but that fizzled out after a few years. The Communists and the MIR were much better organized, and continued to operate until well into the 1990s, long after the end of the dictatorship. Early on I remember the sense of transgression, going to a Communist or a MIR event. Was it wise to cross those lines? Would working with one party compromise our ability to work with another?

Those partisan distinctions and identities were important at first but began to lose their significance by the end of the dictatorship in the 1980s. The military lost a plebiscite in 1988 that asked the country whether they wanted eight more years of Pinochet. I was in Vancouver's La Quena coffee house, in many ways the centre of the Chilean exile community, listening with everyone to reports of the results by long distance phone calls from friends in Chile. We celebrated in joyous disbelief that the dictatorship had lost, and that its end was now in sight.

A year later, after graduating from the University of British Columbia with a BA in political science, I was in Chile for the elections in December 1989 and the transfer of power to a new democratic government in March 1990. Living in Chile during that time had a powerful impact on me. I witnessed the transition to democracy up close, attended rallies, and talked to a broad range of people, including political leaders of all stripes, and shared in the pain and joy of the end of the dictatorship. I was hooked and decided to pursue political science as an academic career.

I also began to understand how much I'd been shaped by growing up as a refugee in the exile community. Exile politics are notoriously black and white. Spending almost a year back in Chile, I saw a much more complex society than the strict good exiles versus evil dictatorship stories I'd grown up with. I spent a lot of time with my extended family, the overwhelming majority of whom had supported the dictatorship, even while seeing us suffer through prison and exile. Some lost faith in the dictatorship soon after the coup, as they saw the brutalities it was committing. Yes, they wanted to stop Chile becoming Marxist, but they were shocked by the horrors of repression.

Others remained firm in their support of Pinochet. For them, he'd saved the country, and they ignored or discounted his atrocities. There were difficult conversations with relatives who barely knew we existed, let alone why we'd been forced to leave. I saw that we'd been written out of their history, and that my presence was a challenge to narratives they'd come to accept. I understood my role as a painful but necessary part of Chile's larger process of coming to terms with its past.

My presence forced some in my family to reassess their narratives, and although I didn't anticipate it, my meeting them began to do the same to me. I came to better understand those who saw the Allende government itself as a threat, who feared that Chile could join the Soviet sphere. I heard stories about how shortly before the coup, the entire family celebrated my uncle's wedding, which was the last time they were together, before everything broke. The conversation turned to politics, not surprisingly, and the fears of an impending armed confrontation. As supporters of the Allende government, my parents were in the minority. My uncle Sergio, afraid of the slide to Marxism he was witnessing, told me that he asked my father whether he thought force would be needed to defend the revolution. "Of course!" was dad's response. "At that point," Sergio told me, "I knew there was no turning back." If someone like my father, whom he loved and respected, had become convinced that force was the only option, the country was irreparably broken and divided. Sergio feared that force would be used against people like him and his family.

I later asked dad about this conversation. Although he didn't remember it exactly, he admitted that yes, he most likely had said this. It was a time of division and conflict, and as a young man he had been swept up. He also confided that in some ways he thought we'd been lucky that the coup happened when it did. If the revolution had continued, instead of victims, perhaps a few years later he and so many others might have become victimizers. Thankfully, we'll never know. I appreciated this frankness, especially from someone who'd been twice victimized, as a Socialist in Chile and as a Jewish child in Europe during the Holocaust.

Hannah Arendt, the political philosopher who wrote much on totalitarianism, knew that under the right circumstances most of us are capable of being complicit in atrocities. It doesn't take monsters to commit evil. In my middle age I've come to appreciate how different circumstances in my childhood might have propelled me and my family down very different paths.

The alternative lives we were spared, thankfully, include those without my father, mother, or both. But they also include alternatives without the coup, where a possibly successful revolution might have victimized my extended instead of my immediate family. My parents have always been driven more by compassion than ideology, and they would likely have been among the first to protest the revolution's excesses instead of lining up to be its victimizers. I'll never know. But many Chileans who did end up in exile in Eastern Europe were shocked by what they saw and expressed that this was not what they had fought for.

Canada had a history of accepting politically friendly refugees from Communist countries like Hungary in 1956 and Czechoslovakia in 1968. The Chileans were the first Marxist refugees, and there was resistance at first to admitting politically risky people from across the Cold War divide. I am of course extremely grateful that Canada took a risk in embracing us. But now it's important for us to bear the heavy burdens of citizenship. That involves, among other things, not perpetuating the myths of refugee victimhood.

Chileans were undoubtedly victimized, like so many other people Canada has admitted. But it's not hard to imagine an alternative history where the moral valences are reversed. We could easily have walked down very different paths. I think of this when I see the debates today over which refugees to admit and how to properly screen them. Victims yes, victimizers absolutely not. While it's true that modern wars regularly target innocent civilians, conflicts in places like Syria, Afghanistan, Sudan, Colombia, the Balkans, or elsewhere, don't sort people out into neat categories. And even though some figures we've come to revere, such as Nelson Mandela, at one point advocated violence, any hint of that on the part of a refugee is likely enough to keep them out of the country. My intention here is not to outline a more effective refugee policy. It's simply to provide a testament that Chilean refugees are as complex and contradictory as anyone. Those complexities and contradictions are not a threat to be avoided, or an embarrassing history to be swept under the rug, but a potential to be better understood. At some point in the future, perhaps, refugees may be able to become citizens without continually demonstrating their victimhood.

After dropping off Irene I headed to my office at CORMU. I was not too worried about the news we had heard of an uprising of the Navy. The Government would be able to take care of the situation.

Traffic was no too bad Probably this September 11 would turn out to be OK...

At the first red light I realized I was terribly wrong!

Although I knew this was a very right wing neighbourhood I was really frightened by the happiness of everybody around me...

...it seemed obvious that this September 11 was going to turn out very much not OK.

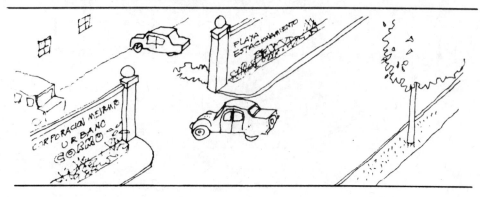

When I arrived there was chaos. Most of CORMU staff loyal to the government was in the central patio (where were those who were against the government is anybody's guess). Although we had expected some kind of a coup for sometime, nobody knew what to do.

CORMU Vicepresident asked me to drive a nurse to Parque San Joaquín to take medical supplies. Much later (already in Canada) I learnt that the Socialist Party command was going to to be there to direct the resistance (that was only sporadic) and that not many that should have been there arrived.

AS IN THE TANQUETAZO

IT IS A MILITARY COUP!!

BUT PINOCHET WAS LOYAL TO THE GOVERNMENT

BUT THE NAVY REBELLED!!

WHAT CAN WE DO? WE HAVE NO WEAPONS!

WITHOUT WEAPONS WE ARE HELPLESS

MAYBE THE ARMY WILL BE LOYAL

ADAM, CAN YOU DRIVE COMPAÑERA CELSA TO PARQUE SAN JOAQUIN? SHE HAS TO TAKE SOME MEDICAL SUPPLIES

On the way we crossed a truckful of soldiers. All had an armband made of kids pajama cloth with a pattern of turtles.

We did not have any problem on our way.

I dropped off Celsa at Parque San Joaquin...

and started my way back to CORMU..

Returning to CORMU was not easy. Although it was only 10 AM the city was already in a state of emergency. Access to downtown from the South was controlled.

There was a carabinero (policeman) blocking cars from going downtown in every street

Fortunately I knew a shortcut through a shanty town that the police had not bothered to block...

...and managed to get behind the roadblocks and eventually get to CORMU

...just on time to listen to the President's last speech. It was 11 AM

Pretty soon it became clear that there was not much for us to do. Around 10 AM we had listened to what clearly was President Allende's last words. He seemed to be aware that to ask the people to defend the government would be a bloodbath. Then the radio (only the government's foe's were stations transmitting) anounced that La Moneda, the presidentialpalace, was going to be bombed.

TWO VERY YOUNG SOLDIERS IN FRONT OF THE CROWD WERE SHOOTING AND ARGUING

THAT NIGHT WE SAT DOWN FOR DINNER LIKE EVERY OTHER NIGHT

BUT OUR LIVES WERE NEVER THE SAME AGAIN

THREE MONTHS LATER
ADAM WAS TAKEN PRISONER.
HE, IRENE AND THEIR CHILDREN PABLO, ANA AND CATALINA
CAME TO CANADA AS REFUGEES AFTER HE WAS RELEASED.
THE PAINTING "MINE SCHWESTER IM CHILE" WAS PAINTED BY
IRENE'S SISTER CECILIA BOISIER
IN GERMANY WHILE ADAM WAS IN PRISON

Floating to the Lure of
the Promised Land
Tamil Refugees in Canada

CYRUS SUNDAR SINGH

In the belly of the cargo ship we held,
Our breath, our noses, and each other.
In the belly of the cargo ship.

A village born of need and circumstance,
Not earth nor roots where we used to stand.

On August 11, 2016, near a small fishing village in Newfoundland, four former
Tamil Sri Lankan refugees—Baskaran, Shanmuga Paul, Siva, and Gandhi—
climbed into an old, beached lifeboat and sat together. Overwhelmed by the
moment, the four men broke down, cried, and comforted each other. The
four were part of a group of 155 Tamil refugees who, in 1986, were set adrift
in two lifeboats for days without food or water, desperately lost somewhere
on the North Atlantic Ocean—no land, no help, no hope.[1] Gandhi recalled

---

1 The exact number of refugees cited in this chapter varies across recollections
and news reports. While these inconsistencies have been preserved, I have chosen

that "for three days, we had no water to drink, no food to eat, and we couldn't move, so we just remained where we sat." Miraculously, on the third day, they were rescued by a local fishing boat whose captain, Gus Dalton, spotted the lifeboats "about ten kilometres west of Saint Shott's on the southern tip of the Avalon Peninsula."[2]

Their story quickly became front-page news in Canada and around the world. That was the first time in recent memory that Canadians had come face to face with Tamils; men, women, and children who were harbingers of the great exodus of thousands of Tamils from Sri Lanka. They sought asylum from a brutal and bloody civil war fought along ethnic lines on the small island nation off the southern tip of India. Over the course of a decade, more than half a million Tamil civilians fled the country to India, Russia, Germany, France, Italy, the United Kingdom, and Australia. And they also came to Canada because it was known to have a history of providing safe haven for those who were escaping violence. Or did it?

On December 10, 2015, the day on which the first Syrian refugees arrived at Toronto's Pearson Airport, the *Toronto Star* splashed a bold headline across its front page: "WELCOME TO CANADA." The headline was accompanied by a photograph of a young boy, clad in a red-and-white striped T-shirt, shorts, and a cowboy hat, running through a grassy field holding a large Canadian flag above his head, billowing out behind him. *"Ahlan wa sahlan,"* the article began. "You're with family now. And your presence among us makes our Christmas season of peace and joy just that much brighter." It went on to say, "It's been a long trek, but you are no longer refugees. Your days of being strangers in a strange land are over."[3]

Some thirty years earlier, the same newspaper had run the following story:

to use 155—the number given, for example, in a relatively recent *Maclean's* article that recounts the events of 1986. See Lyndsay Jones, "How a Newfoundland Fisherman Became Godfather to a Generation of Tamil Canadians," *Maclean's*, January 31, 2018.

2 Commentary by Kathryn Wright, "Sri Lankan Migrants Rescued off Newfoundland," *The National*, with Knowlton Nash, CBC Television, August 12, 1986, http://www.cbc.ca/player/play/1707584996.

3 "Welcome to Canada," *Toronto Star*, December 10, 2015, https://www.pressreader.com/canada/toronto-star/20151210/281479275354062.

More than 150 Sri Lankan men, women and children, found adrift off the coast of Newfoundland in crammed open lifeboats yesterday, arrived safely in port here this morning after being rescued by Canadian fishermen. As startled immigration officials here and in Ottawa pondered what to do with this unprecedented load of alleged refugees, the 152 castaways claimed they are Tamils fleeing persecution in strife-torn Sri Lanka.[4]

The words "alleged," "claimed," "startled," and "unprecedented load" are notable and markedly different from the tone of the *Toronto Star* headline of 2015.

One of the refugees in that overcrowded lifeboat spoke with me in the winter of 2016, providing personal testimony of his experiences fleeing Sri Lanka, his time in the lifeboat, and his years toiling in the kitchens of Toronto restaurants. He asked that I not use his name because he was ashamed, so I will call him "Anonymous":

Although it has been thirty years since we arrived, I still feel ashamed. If we had arrived by airplane, we would feel better. In the early days, the white people would shame us for arriving on a boat. They called us "boat people" and used it as a demeaning and subjugating term. I worked in kitchens as a prep cook and got into many arguments with the bosses about the condition of our arrival. I tried to tell them the story, but they did not want to hear it. They accused us of being so poor that we were opportunists who jumped the queue for a better life. We did not *want* to leave—we *had* to leave or die![5]

He was not alone in this shame. The Tamil boat people were greeted by a significant amount of backlash. People wrote letters to leading newspapers denouncing them, with many writers urging the government to "send the Tamils back where they came from." One reader went to the extreme of

4 Alan Story and Joseph Hall, "152 Castaways Paid Thousands to Flee to Canada," *Toronto Star*, August 12, 1986.

5 Transcribed interview notes from a conversation, in Tamil, with the author held in Toronto on April 4, 2016; here and elsewhere, all translations are my own. This interview, from which I quote further below, was among those I conducted for my live documentary *Brothers in the Kitchen* (2016), which was performed on May 4, 2016, in Toronto. For the final script, see Cyrus Sundar Singh, "Brothers in the Kitchen: The Uprising, Exodus and Survival of a Tamil Minority," MFA thesis, Ryerson University, 2016, 45–77.

suggesting in his letter to the *Toronto Sun* that the Canadian government should have "sunken the lifeboats."[6] Furthermore, these refugees were shamed from within their own community. Although Tamil Canadians in Montréal and Toronto offered assistance, others within the community thought that the boat people had improperly jumped the queue, lied to Canadian authorities, and had paid large sums of money to be smuggled here, giving all Tamil Canadians a bad name. Many within the community distanced themselves from those who had arrived in the lifeboats. As time passed, a cloud of shame grew around the lifeboat, its journey, and the Tamil boat people.

Since the 1980s, Sri Lanka, formerly known as Ceylon, had been embroiled in a protracted and devastating civil war that had polarized its citizens along ethnic lines—a Sinhalese Buddhist majority and a Tamil Hindu minority. After the nation's independence from Britain in 1948, the majority Sinhalese expressed pent-up hostilities toward the minority Tamils by passing several highly discriminatory regulations. In response, Tamils agitated for a separate state. Tensions exploded into ongoing, communal violence that resulted in tremendous casualties and suffering on both sides. In 1956, for example, violence erupted when Sinhala was made the official language under the Sinhala Only Act. Further riots occurred in 1958, after an agreement partially rescinding the ban on Tamil as an official language was revoked. Perhaps as many as 1,500 Tamils were slaughtered, and many thousands displaced.[7] Recollecting those events, Toronto Tamil elder Sri Guggan Sri-Skanda-Rajah described an unforgettable day:

> On May 25, 1958, when I was 15 years old, seventy Tamil people sought refuge at my parents' home in the outskirts of Colombo. They were running away from a Sinhalese mob of about 3,000 looking for blood. They

6 Selva Ponnuchami, "Rescue of 155 Tamil Refugees from Two Lifeboats off the Coast of Newfoundland: Thirty Years Ago . . ." *Monsoon Journal,* July 2016, https://issuu.com/monsoonjournal/docs/mj_july_2016_web, p. 19. Ponnuchami was the president of the Eelam Tamil Association of Quebec at the time the refugees arrived.

7 "Massacres, Pogroms, Destruction of Property, Sexual Violence and Assassinations of Civil Society Leaders," International Human Rights Association Bremen, submission to the Permanent Peoples' Tribunal, second session of the Peoples' Tribunal on Sri Lanka, Bremen, December 7–10, 2013, http://www.ptsrilanka.org/pogroms-and-massacres/, 7.

were finally rescued by a platoon of [Sinhalese] Army volunteers. They first saved the women and children and then came back for the men.[8]

The conflict continued for decades, marked by bouts of violence through the late 1960s, 1970s, and in 1983, Army volunteers disarmed the Tamils and instead of offering them protection as they had done in 1958, handed the Tamils over to the Sinhalese rioters. The ongoing oppressive conditions and subjugation laid the foundation for armed uprisings by many Tamil resistance/guerrilla groups, each vying for superiority. Eventually, in 1976, the Liberation Tigers of Tamil Eelam (LTTE)—commonly known as the Tamil Tigers—rose to prominence with the goal of establishing Tamil Eelam, an independent Tamil state in northern and eastern Sri Lanka. On July 23, 1983, when the LTTE killed thirteen Sri Lankan Army soldiers in a planned ambush, all hell broke loose and ignited the defining deadly riots known as Black July.

From Sunday, July 24, to Saturday, July 30, Colombo, the cosmopolitan capital city, was the centre of looting, killing, and ethnic cleansing. Spurred on by nationalist Sinhala-Buddhist fervour, mobs of Sinhalese men armed with knives, steel rods, and machetes, roamed the streets looking for blood. They were also armed with electoral voter lists that showed where the Tamil homes were located. For seven days and nights, Tamil-owned shops, businesses, homes, and Tamils themselves were the targets of heinous crimes. Numerous eyewitness accounts exist of Tamil women and girls who were gang-raped by mobs, then brutally killed or set on fire or by other brutalities, including decapitation.[9]

Black July sparked the mass exodus of mostly young Tamil men whose future held either a rebel uniform, a prisoner of the state uniform, or death. Those who had the means fled the island nation by any means necessary. Anonymous told me that his family had found the money to pay for a plane

---

8 Interview with the author, April 23, 2004, Toronto.

9 See Eleanor Pavey, "The Massacres in Sri Lanka During the Black July Riots of 1983," May 13, 2008, *Online Encyclopedia of Mass Violence*, Mass Violence and Resistance Research Network, Sciences Po, https://www.sciencespo.fr/mass-violence-war-massacre-resistance/en/document/massacres-sri-lanka-during-black-july-riots-1983. For a chronology, see "Events of Black July," *Black July '83: Remembering Silenced Voices* (website), 2009, http://www.blackjuly83.com/EventsofBlackJuly.htm.

ticket on a flight out of Sri Lanka, but first he had to travel by bus from his home in Jaffna, on the northern tip of the island, to the airport in Colombo, some 400 kilometres south. The people on the bus were all Tamil, and he was the youngest. There were several Sinhalese checkpoints along the route, and he recounted to me the day the bus was stopped at one checkpoint and they were all ordered to get off the bus:

> The soldiers separated me and put a gun to my chest. They wanted to kill me. They asked me to show my ID. So I held up the ID with both my hands. The ID was in Tamil, Sinhala and English but the Sinhala soldier could not read at all. So, in frustration he hit me, hard. He then asked a Muslim soldier to translate. I told them that I was a businessman, and I was going to Colombo to have my passport renewed. This was all translated to the Sinhalese soldier by the Muslim soldier. The Sinhala soldier then ordered me to run and to not look back. I began to run saying, "Please don't shoot!" I ran for dear life because they kept shooting to scare me. They had also ordered the bus driver to get going without me. So, I ran alongside the bus and eventually managed to get back on the bus.

Tamils took circuitous routes through many Eastern Bloc countries that during that time did not require visas for entry, such as the Soviet Union, Czechoslovakia, and East Germany, where the Berlin Wall was still in place. His recollection continued:

> I flew to Berlin, East Germany. Back then we did not need visas for East Germany. In Berlin we made a run for it across the Berlin Wall and crossed over in the middle of the night. Then by train into West Germany, where I claimed refugee status and was sent to a refugee camp. I spent 22 months in Germany in a refugee camp. We were not allowed to move around too much and could not work. I learned to cook in the refugee camps.

The Tamils lived under rigid regulations in West German refugee compounds. Although they were housed and received social assistance, they were prevented from seeking employment, had travel restrictions, and were not allowed to study. The refugees also feared the possibility that the West German government, who viewed these Tamils as economic refugees, would deport them back to Sri Lanka. In an interview published in the October

1986 issue of the journal *Refuge*, Sri-Skanda-Rajah asserted that "faced with the prospect of forcible removal back to Sri Lanka or to some other unknown place and the accompanying danger and uncertainty this prospect posed, the Tamils chose to come to Canada by surreptitious means."[10]

As Anonymous explained, word spread through the refugee compound that an agent could arrange passage on a German freighter that was ready to smuggle them to Canada. The total cost, he said, was 5,000 Deutsche Marks, with 3,000 to be paid to the agent before boarding, and the rest upon arrival in Canada. The refugees somehow found the money and bought hope as passengers on board a 424-ton freighter named the *Aurigae*, owned and operated by Wolfgang Bindel, a West German citizen.[11] The journey began on a late July afternoon. They were herded into a minivan on the way to the ship that would take them to a new land and their new lives. Late that night, under the cloak of darkness, the *Aurigae* left the Weser River port of Brake, north of Bremen, Germany with all their fears, hopes, and dreams illegally packed inside. They were promised rooms, beds, food, water, and a good journey and told that they would reach Canada in three to four days. He continued his story:

> All of this was a lie. As we found out none of this was true. We were 156 strangers who boarded that ship in Germany. For eleven days, we are sitting in fear in the cargo ship. All 156 passengers survived on the floor of the ship. We were all strangers. There were three or four women and a few children. The bread went mouldy in a few days so we had to just cook rice and frozen chicken or a simple congee. Our people cooked together. People were getting sick and some threw up. The ship was very

---

10 "An Interview on the Case of the 155 Tamil Refugees," *Refuge* 6, no. 1 (1986): 8–9, https://refuge.journals.yorku.ca/index.php/refuge/article/view/21493, 8. At the time, Sri-Skanda-Rajah was a community legal aid worker in Toronto and vice-chair of the Toronto Refugee Affairs Council.

11 James M. Markham, "Tamils off Canada Fled Germany, Police Say," *New York Times*, August 16, 1986, https://www.nytimes.com/1986/08/16/world/tamils-off-canada-fled-germany-police-say.html. Unsurprisingly, Bindel told a different story: see James M. Markham, "German Captain Denies Role in Tamils' Journey, *New York Times*, August 17, 1986, http://www.nytimes.com/1986/08/17/world/german-captain-denies-role-in-tamils-journey.html. See also Andrew Maykuth, "Unraveling the Mystery of Tamils' Flight to Canada," *Philadelphia Inquirer*, August 17, 1986, http://www.maykuth.com/archives/tamil86.htm.

dirty. We were all on the floor all the time. No beds, no berth, no comfort. We were refugees.

Fourteen days later, with only the clothes on their backs, Bindel forced them off the *Aurigae* into two lifeboats somewhere in the North Atlantic. Adrift for days without food or water and with no land in sight, they were ready to jump overboard into the salty seas, and some of them made a suicide pact. The panicked mother and father of a six-month-old baby were among those making death pacts, ready to plunge to their end. Gandhi remembered the moment:

> The boat was full of water, and we thought that we were all going to die.
> When the six-month-old baby had cried itself into silence, we thought
> the baby had died. The mother of the baby vowed that, if her baby dies,
> she would jump into the water and kill herself. The father and mother
> were seated next to me, so I consoled them by saying that we had all
> taken a huge chance, travelled a long distance, and paid huge sums of
> money to come to Canada and that we should continue to keep our faith
> that we will reach Canada. For three days, we had no water to drink,
> no food to eat, and we couldn't move, so we just remained where we
> sat. And I'm even ashamed to speak about this now but we even had to
> defecate just where we sat.[12]

Out in the gentle swells just outside St. Mary's Bay, Newfoundland, the fishing longboat, the *Atlantic Reaper*, steamed alongside two open lifeboats that were joined together by a simple rope. Squinting through the fog, Gus Dalton, the skipper, eyed the strange cargo: scores of people, black-haired and dark-skinned. Huddled together and waterlogged were 155 people in two boats designed to carry thirty-five each. "You couldn't see between them— they was so crowded," remarked Dalton. "All I could see was heads. I figured they was boat people."[13]

Most surprising—and heart wrenching—was how young many of the castaways were. Some were barely out of their teens. They were young men who had been separated from their parents for the first time because their

12 Tape-recorded interview, in Tamil, with Annalingam Suhapiranan (a.k.a. "Gandhi"), August 12, 2016, in St. John's, Newfoundland.
13 Quoted in Alan Story and Joseph Hall, "152 Castaways Paid Thousands to Flee to Canada," *Toronto Star*, August 12, 1986.

very age and gender made them more vulnerable as potential recruits for the Tamil anti-government militants and therefore as targets of the state security forces. "The consideration of our families was that we should be sent away so that at least one survives," said Ramanathan, one of the Tamil refugees who had sought passage on the *Aurigae*. He added that "we had heard of and seen friends taken away by the Army to the camps, so I wanted to go out of the country."[14]

When they arrived in St. John's, Newfoundland, they faced many questions. Where had they come from? How did they manage the Atlantic crossing? Who set them adrift with no food and water in crammed lifeboats? How did they manage to survive for days out on the open sea? It didn't take long for many, often contradictory, versions of events to emerge. Once again, Tamil elder Sri-Skanda-Rajah provided some context:

> It was natural that they would want to take the steps necessary to ensure their safety and security. It is only in light of these extenuating circumstances that their actions can be understood. Unfortunately, the method they chose, and the story they decided to tell, adversely affected their reception in Canada.[15]

Despite the many uncertainties and remaining questions about their arrival, then Canadian Prime Minister Brian Mulroney granted the Tamils one-year ministerial permits to stay and work. Furthermore, in response to criticism and calls for immigration reform, he emphasized that the need for reform was separate from the question of whether or not Canada would offer protection to refugees who arrived on its shores. Mulroney sent a clear message with his statement that "Canada was built by immigrants and refugees, and those who arrive in lifeboats off our shores are not going to be turned away."[16]

---

14 Quoted in Paul Watson and Paula Todd, "Tamils' Lot: Hard Work Long Hours," *Toronto Star*, August 11, 1987.

15 "An Interview on the Case of the 155 Tamil Refugees," 8.

16 Quoted in Jeff Bradley, "Prime Minister Vows That Sri Lankans Will Not Be Turned Away," *AP News*, August 18, 1986, https://apnews.com/538dc177df-174766db50320868938c30. See also Alexandra Mann, "Refugees Who Arrive by Boat and Canada's Commitment to the Refugee Convention: A Discursive Analysis," *Refuge* 26, no. 2 (2009): 191–206, https://refuge.journals.yorku.ca/index.php/refuge/article/view/32088, esp. 197–98.

For many Tamil refugees who arrived in Toronto during this time, their first home was the downtown community of St. James Town, an area full of high-rise apartments that proudly described itself as "the most densely populated neighbourhood in Canada."[17] It was also just a few blocks from my home in the 1980s. In those early days, almost all Tamil refugees were young single men. They had to survive. They worked multiple shifts, lived together in groups to cut costs, and shared beds on a rotating schedule.[18] Once these young men had jobs, they sent portions of their earnings back home to pay off debts—usually incurred to make the journey to Canada—and to help their families. Soon, Tamil-owned retail businesses flourished in the vicinity of my neighbourhood, helping to revitalize a depressed area. Since their sizable population required culturally specific goods and services, the entrepreneurs in the community opened grocery and clothing stores, bookshops and libraries, newspapers, radio and television stations, temples, and churches.

It wasn't long before I noticed brown-skinned brothers working in the kitchens of Toronto's bustling restaurant scene. They washed dishes, cleaned tables, and cooked behind the scenes. Although they remained invisible beyond the kitchens, their culinary skills were visible on the plates of discriminating restaurant patrons. They cooked every food imaginable: from risotto to ratatouille, brisket to Bolognese. These brown-skinned brothers infiltrated the restaurant industry—but only through the back doors. I noticed they were not on the front lines as hosts, waiters, or bartenders, and remained away from direct contact with clientele. I wondered if this was by circumstance or design. I wanted to explore and understand their struggle, displacement, migration, settlement, and agitation, at least by some, for the restoration of a Tamil homeland—Tamil Eelam—on the island of Sri Lanka. Since the crushing of the Tamil Tigers by the Sri Lankan military in 2009, the struggle had continued, even in the diaspora.[19]

17 "About the Neighbourhood," St. James Town: A World Within a Block, accessed July 10, 2020, https://www.stjamestown.org/the-neighbourhood/#about-SJT.

18 Leonie Sandercock, *The Quest for an Inclusive City: An Exploration of Sri Lankan Tamil Experience of Integration in Toronto and Vancouver*, Working Paper no. 04–12, May 2004 (Burnaby, BC: Vancouver Centre of Excellence for Research on Immigration and Integration in the Metropolis, 2004), 12–13.

19 As poet and scholar Rudhramoorthy Cheran pointed out in 2013, "The demand for the recognition of Tamil as a nation is present in current articulations by the

This exploration led me toward the initial research for a documentary film about the Tamil Sri Lankan diaspora's journey to Canada. Despite some progress in locating a significant number of people who sought refuge in those lifeboats in 1986, I encountered problems. For many the topic was taboo. There was much fear and mistrust in the air. Though all 155 Tamil refugees rescued from the lifeboats were granted special ministerial permits, which allowed them to stay and work in Canada, most were highly reticent to tell their stories on camera. As the war in Sri Lanka was actively raging in the early years of the twenty-first century, the former refugees feared for their lives and for the safety of loved ones back home, or were afraid of being deported for entering Canada illegally. Still others feared intimidation by the Tamil Tigers, whose Toronto representatives engaged in sometimes aggressive fundraising activities.[20] In the early days, even my research interviews with subjects in the Tamil Canadian community generated allegations that I was a spy for the Indian Army. Some subjects agreed to do interviews but then denied permission for me to use them afterwards. Others agreed only to audio interviews without identification to retain their anonymity.

Nobody seemed to see this project as valuable or interesting, including broadcasters and the National Film Board of Canada. After several years and much work, I became discouraged and demoralized. I had reached a dead end. Faced with the economic pressures of sustaining a small independent production company and coupled with the broadcast industry's lack of interest in the "Tamil Sri Lankan" subject, prospects of moving forward with this production were bleak. With regret, I placed the project on the back burner. A dozen years later, I seized an extraordinary opportunity through a Master of Fine Arts (MFA) documentary media program at Ryerson University and

---

Tamil National Alliance and other Tamil parties, even though they are willing to live under a united Sri Lanka. This has become their discourse. But the contradiction is that the Tamil nation has become a 'transnation' because, while they have been fighting for territory, almost a million and a half Tamils have left the country, and the exodus continues." "On Responsible Distance: An Interview with R. Cheran by Aparne Halpé," *University of Toronto Quarterly* 84, no. 4 (Fall 2015): 90–108.

20 See Amarnath Amarasingam, *Pain, Pride, and Politics: Social Movement Activism and the Sri Lankan Diaspora in Canada* (Athens: University of Georgia Press, 2015), pp. 1–2; "Tamil Tigers," *CBC News*, April 20, 2009, updated May 19, 2009, http://www.cbc.ca/news/canada/tamil-tigers-1.783483.

revived the journey of the Tamil Sri Lankan diaspora as my thesis documentary project.

I began my research anew but quickly realized that with the passage of time (three decades since the first arrival of the Tamil refugees), the stories had changed, and so had I. And there were new stories—those who moved beyond the Sri Lankan trauma into a fresh twenty-first-century start in Canada. I envisioned a hybrid between a site-specific performance and a live documentary during which the primary documentary subjects and the audience would be present inside a site integral to the story, in this case a café. *Brothers in the Kitchen* premiered as part of the Hot Docs Canadian International Documentary Festival in May 2016. On that night, thirteen subjects of the documentary, who were people of all ages, amateurs and professionals, authors and politicians, told their stories live to an audience seated within the same space.

Leading up to that documentary festival premiere, in January 2016 I was also involved in both the planning and execution of an important reunion in Newfoundland to mark the 30th anniversary of the arrival and rescue of the 155 Tamil refugees off the Avalon peninsula in August 1986. I was given exclusive access to document the process and, as a member of the planning committee, I actively participated by sharing my research, ideas, connections, and know-how. In fact, I profoundly influenced the story, and even changed history: as a result of my ongoing independent research, I located one of the two original lifeboats in which the Tamil refugees had arrived. I advocated for the lifeboat's inclusion in the reunion itinerary, and the lifeboat became the centrepiece of that reunion. Sometimes, the stars align and offer fantastical gifts. The seeds I had planted years earlier as part of my research came to fruition at this reunion. Akin to what NHL hockey fans refer to as a "hat trick" (when a player scores three goals in a single game), three incredible touchstones were the gifts to the reunion.

On August 11, 2016, a yellow school bus filled with a large group of Tamil Canadians, former and current Canadian MPs, my documentary film crew, journalists, and friends left St. John's, Newfoundland, and headed south toward the small fishing village of Holyrood on the Avalon Peninsula. There, four former Tamil Sri Lankan refugees—Baskaran, Shanmuga Paul, Siva, and Gandhi—were reunited with one of the two lifeboats in which they and the other passengers on the *Aurigae* had been set adrift three decades earlier. That powerful moment was not only witnessed by those present but also by thousands of virtual onlookers through tweets, blogs, and texts. At least sixteen print media outlets from coast to coast, as well as national broadcasters CBC and CTV, covered the story.

The entire entourage then travelled farther south to St. Mary's Bay and reunited with retired fisherman Captain Gus Dalton, who had found and rescued the refugees on the same date back in 1986. After many tears, reminiscing, lunch, and cake, we returned to St. John's for a news conference on board the Canadian Coast Guard (CCG) ship *Leonard J. Cowley*, which had arrived in St. John's for refuelling. This was the same CCG ship that had picked up the refugees rescued by Captain Gus Dalton and had brought them to St. John's. In addition, the press conference was hosted by CCG Assistant Commissioner Wade Spurrell, who welcomed the refugees back to where they'd first made landfall thirty years ago. He was the chief officer on the *Leonard J. Cowley* and was aboard the night they picked up the Tamil refugees. "Men and women of the Canadian Coast Guard often have a chance to help mariners and people in distress on the water," Spurrell stated, noting that only very rarely "do people come back to see us, so this is very remarkable for us."[21] My documentary research connected me directly to the CCG and to the assistant commissioner, whom I had met with the day before and planned the subsequent press conference.

Interestingly, there was a related story unfolding involving the community, its leaders, and the storyteller. It was a delicate negotiation between what the community wanted to show, what the leaders wanted to shape, and what this storyteller wanted to reveal. It was then that I understood that the story and the lifeboat were larger than me. The boat had become a symbol that closed the circle and celebrated the community. Without consultation with me or with any of the Tamils who were passengers on the lifeboat, the Canadian Tamil Congress (CTC), which organized the reunion in Newfoundland, purchased the lifeboat, transported it to Toronto, and proudly displayed it at Tamilfest—the Tamil Street Festival in Scarborough held at the end of August 2016. Consciously or unconsciously, the CTC used the lifeboat as a tool to legitimize the community's arrival narrative. The boat came to symbolize the Tamil refugees and has taken on new meaning for the Tamil

---

21 Quoted in "Tamil Refugees Revisit N.L. Rescuers 30 Years Later," *The Telegram*, August 11, 2016, http://www.thetelegram.com/news/local/tamil-refugees-revisit-nl-rescuers-30-years-later-127504/.

Sri Lankan community and Canadians at large. It has also given Canada a second chance to properly welcome the Tamil refugees and embrace the community.

In August 2010, ten months after a Thai ship, the *Ocean Lady*, had arrived on the west coast with 76 Tamil refugees on board, another Thai cargo ship named the *Sun Sea* appeared off the coast of Vancouver Island with 492 Sri Lankan Tamil refugees on board. Back in August 1986, Prime Minister Brian Mulroney had offered comforting words, assistance, and ministerial permits to a similar group of refugees. Under the government of Prime Minister Stephen Harper, Canada's welcome to these asylum seekers was very different, as a Canadian Council for Refugees report on the two incidents notes:

> The passengers [of both ships] were subjected by the government to prolonged detention, intensive interrogation and energetic efforts to exclude them from the refugee process, or to contest their claim if they succeeded in entering the refugee process. Canada's immigration legislation was amended to give the government extraordinary new powers, many apparently unconstitutional, to detain people and deny them a wide range of rights. [. . .] There was loud and strident public messaging about the alleged dangers presented by the arrival of the passengers. Yet, few have been found to represent any kind of security concern and almost two-thirds of the passengers whose claims have been heard have been found to be refugees in need of Canada's protection.

The trend continued. Five years after the arrival of the *Sun Sea*, Canada had "dramatically closed its doors on refugees, breached its international human rights obligations, and lost its reputation as a world leader in refugee protection."[22]

When I invited my anonymous confidant to join the other former passengers of the lifeboat at Tamilfest as a proud ambassador, or at least as a silent witness to the changing reception of the lifeboat, he declined, still too ashamed to come, for fear of revealing his origins as an illegal immigrant (as he described himself), or simply as a lowly boat person who ended up in a kitchen. I have let him have the last say:

22 Canadian Council for Refugees, *Sun Sea: Five Years Later*, August 2015, https://ccrweb.ca/sites/ccrweb.ca/files/sun-sea-five-years-later.pdf, 1.

I'm the only one in my family that left Sri Lanka. I went back in 1994 to get married. Up till that time I was a supporter of the Tamil rebels, but what I witnessed in Jaffna during that time. I no longer support any side. Our Tamil people were *used* for the drama of the civil war, and we have paid a heavy price. I'm no longer interested in a fucking Tamil Eelam. This is my home now. I'll die in Canada. I got married, and we have two children. My children would like to visit Sri Lanka but not live there. Their lives are also in Canada. I am so grateful for the government of Brian Mulroney. He was good to us.

"I still hate the term 'boat people,'" he added. "I do not want to be known by that name."

Refugee Children in Canadian Schools

The Role of Teachers in
Supporting Integration and Inclusion

CHRISTINA PARKER

A teacher asked her Grade 5 class: "What are some of the reasons for moving to Canada?" Ten-year-old Jamal, who had recently emigrated from Kenya, readily responded to this question: "War. It's too dangerous." Others said: "better job," "education," "better opportunities," "they want peace," "they want new things," "the government is not treating them well," "freedom to practice their religion," "a multicultural country where everyone is respected." The teacher then asked, "What does *refugees* mean?" Caden, a Chinese boy whose mother had initially been denied entry into Canada, responded, "It means they do not feel safe, and then decide to come here as a refugee to live here."[1] I observed this lesson on immigrants and refugees in Canada as part of my ethnographic study of children's experiences with peacebuilding education in Canadian schools. Throughout this chapter, I draw on my experiences as

---

1 These comments were made in March 2011, in a Grade 5 classroom in Toronto. I was present at the time as a classroom observer. For additional discussion, see Christina Parker, *Peacebuilding, Citizenship, and Identity: Empowering Conflict and Dialogue in Multicultural Classrooms* (Rotterdam: Sense, 2016), esp. chap. 4, "Identity Connections: Conflictual Issues Across Time, Space, and Culture."

a researcher and teacher to discern the experiences of refugee children and their families navigating the complex system of schooling.

Children are acutely aware of conflict and trauma; they have their own interpretations and perceptions of immigration and belonging in Canada. The students in this teacher's class were all students of colour and had been in Canada for one generation or less. Their teacher, an immigrant from India, appeared to be comfortable posing questions about immigration to Canada. In their unit of study on immigration, the teacher told her students to ask their parents about why people moved to a new country and why they had come to Canada. Drawing on the textbook, the teacher explained the differences between the government's "family" and "refugee" classes of immigrant. Many students were personally familiar with the latter.

Many teachers in urban—and some rural—settings have recently experienced a greater number of refugee students in their classrooms. Canada accepted more than 321,035 permanent residents in 2018, and more than 62,000 of those had been admitted on various humanitarian grounds. This figure included upwards of 46,000 resettled refugees. Close to half of these resettled refugees—nearly 22,000—were under eighteen.[2]

Across Canada, elementary school social studies curricula include a unit on immigration to Canada; in Ontario, students study this topic in Grade 5. The presence of immigrant and refugee students in Canadian classrooms influences how students connect with the curriculum, each other, and the school community. The experiences of refugee students are varied, as are the experiences that teachers have with refugee students in their classroom. One Toronto teacher attempted to engage with his diverse Grade 3 students' cultural histories. During a discussion about a folktale, he mistakenly assumed that one of his students, an Afghani, was from Pakistan. The student, who had spent a year at a Pakistani refugee camp, was hurt, and retorted, "I'm not from Pakistan."[3] Like this student, others might be sensitive to discussions that highlight their perceived ethnicity and experiences based on stereotypes.

2 Immigration, Refugees and Citizenship Canada, *2019 Annual Report to Parliament on Immigration*, Government of Canada, last modified November 1, 2019, https://www.canada.ca/content/dam/ircc/migration/ircc/english/pdf/pub/annual-report-2019.pdf, p. 3.

3 Curt Dudley-Marling, "'I'm Not from Pakistan': Multicultural Literature and the Problem of Representation," *The New Advocate* 10 (1997): 123–34.

Refugee children who have emigrated from conflict zones are usually dealing with multiple challenges and issues that affect their integration into school. For instance, their not being able to speak the same language as their peers, their exposure to violence in their country of origin, and their being separated from family members all impact children's mental health and well-being.[4] Many who have spent time in a refugee camp have not had access to schooling, and others have experienced substantial learning disruptions. Such issues need to be addressed so that students with violent and traumatic histories can receive the kind of support that will allow them to successfully integrate and participate in school. Refugee students with marginalized backgrounds also have a higher probability of encountering instances of conflict at school with students, teachers, and the school system.[5] They have the potential for higher levels of social and academic disengagement, possibly resulting in disproportionately fewer refugee students completing school in Canada. Schools are a unique and ideal resource for refugee families, and with adequate resources and support, they have the capacity to offer programming and services for children and their parents. The day-to-day classroom experience for refugee children is pivotal for successfully learning new cultural norms and practices. Teachers obviously play a key part in these students' integration.

TEACHERS' SUBJECTIVE IDENTITIES

In my experience as an elementary teacher, teacher educator, and researcher in diverse schools in Toronto, Canada, I have worked in many schools in areas characterized as high priority with marginalized populations; most of the students have been in Canada for one generation or less. I have spent

---

4 Katie Stadelman, "Caring for Kids New to Canada: Mental Health Promotion," Canadian Paediatric Society, April 2019, https://www.kidsnewtocanada.ca/mental-health/mental-health-promotion.

5 See, for example, Motoko Akiba, "Predictors of Student Fear of School Violence: A Comparative Study of Eighth Graders in 33 Countries," *School Effectiveness and School Improvement* 19, no. 1 (2008): 51–72; Kent Spencer and Ian Austin, "Gangs a Threat to Refugee Kids," *The Province* (Vancouver), November 10, 2011; Hieu Van Ngo, Avery Calhoun, Catherine Worthington, Tim Pyrch, and David Este, "The Unravelling of Identities and Belonging: Criminal Gang Involvement of Youth from Immigrant Families," *Journal of International Migration and Integration* 18, no. 1 (2017): 63–84.

significant amounts of time in a range of different classrooms, training teachers, learning from teachers, and conducting research with children and youth. My identity shapes how I work with students and teachers because my subjectivity as a teacher and researcher ultimately reflects my own history and culture. My position as a second-generation immigrant-settler in Canada may at times provide me with a privileged understanding of my participants. Still, even though I witnessed my parents' immigration experiences, their cultural navigation and assimilation process is not and never will be the same as that of the varying students and teachers I work with, who all come with their own perceptions and experiences with migration. I cannot presume that I understand them simply because of my own generational history of immigration. Furthermore, students and teachers' identities, such as citizenship status, race, ethnicity, class, and gender identities complicate their individual histories and experiences.

A large part of my work has been concerned with the integration of newcomer immigrant and refugee children into school. I have focused on how these students connect to the curriculum and on how some of their lived histories and experiences with conflict, war, and trauma have affected their engagement at school. In my work training novice teachers, I have had mixed results. Some teachers have felt equipped and ready to engage in the kind of cultural learning that is necessary for dealing with immigrant and refugee students' experiences, while others hold on tightly to Westernized social and cultural lenses that inhibit their understanding of cultural differences.

Having a new student come into the classroom creates change and sometimes disruption. Schools are filled with disruptions, and teachers are expected to instinctively know how to handle them. Teachers acclimatizing new students to the classroom might ask them to share their name, get them set up with a new desk and notebook, and then continue their day-to-day role as teachers. However, what happens when such students do not speak English, and are perhaps carrying trauma from having just come from a refugee camp?

In the schools where I have worked as either a teacher or researcher, many administrators and teachers have expressed frustration with newcomer parents refusing to have their child tested or assessed for various learning abilities. They argue that newcomer parents fear that these assessments will lead to further isolation for their children, that they may be separated from their peers in mainstream classrooms, or become withdrawn. The parents have a point: while many of these assessments can lead to further support and access to resources, they can also further marginalize children who are already in marginalized positions. Communications around fears such as this are often unaddressed.

Many teachers (and their students) do not feel prepared to address conflicts that may arise from diversity in their classrooms, particularly as this diversity relates to race, culture, gender, and religion. For instance, what respect and being "polite" looks like is different in different cultures, which often results in conflict between students and teachers. This is particularly heightened for female students, where societal expectations of model politeness are often conflated and misconstrued. In one case, a teacher felt that her students were constantly disrespecting her because they avoided making eye contact with her when she spoke to them. Only much later in the school year did she realize that her students (mostly of South Asian background) were trying to show her respect.[6] In another classroom that I observed, Anya arrived from Pakistan at her new Grade 4 classroom. She came dressed in her cultural attire and sat quietly in the seat that her teacher pointed out to her. When her teacher called upon her to respond to a question, she quietly stood up and looked straight ahead to verbalize her response. Many of the students, most of whom carried immigrant histories themselves, snickered. The teacher herself let out a little giggle. Mocking Anya illustrated the complexity of the acculturation process that children experience. In the context that Anya migrated from, it was a social norm and expectation to respond to her teacher in this way; however, as her acculturation journey was just beginning, she still lacked the cultural knowledge and social norms of how children were expected to behave in Canadian schools.

DISCUSSING CONFLICTUAL AND SENSITIVE ISSUES

Refugees' lived experiences are difficult to discuss, name, or acknowledge, particularly for children; similarly, it is often uncomfortable for teachers, who may feel inadequate and unprepared to engage in such dialogue. Inviting students from marginalized backgrounds to speak often allows them

---

6 Christina Parker and Kathy Bickmore, "Conflict Management and Dialogue with Diverse Students: Novice Teachers' Approaches and Concerns," *Journal of Teaching and Learning* 8, no. 2 (2012): 47–64.

to feel included. However, discussing sensitive issues can be detrimental to classroom social relations if adequate preparations have not been made.

In one Grade 4 classroom where I spent a significant amount of time learning and researching, I met Swetha, who had emigrated with her parents as refugees from Sri Lanka. From experience, she knew the difference between countries at war and countries at peace, but it was not something that she raised in the class. There, she chose to articulate her family's happiness about their arrival. However, because of her close connection to Sri Lanka and her awareness of political unrest, she was perhaps more aware than many others in her class about what it meant to actually live in what she perceived to be a peaceful country.

The Sri Lankan civil war was a contentious issue in the news at the time I met her. The war had ended in May 2009 after the Mullivaikkal massacre, in which well over forty thousand Tamils died, following which the Sinhala government proclaimed victory. In August 2010, nearly five hundred Tamil Sri Lankans had arrived in Canada by boat, seeking refugee status or some other form of official protection. They were placed in detention, and the government of Stephen Harper made considerable efforts to prevent them from remaining in Canada. This was Swetha's family's experience, as she revealed to me in an interview:

> In my parents' home country . . . in Sri Lanka nowadays there is, like, armies and . . . they're, like, shooting only the Tamil people and Tamil people are dying . . . but the government of Sri Lanka is the one that's telling them to do it because he's Sinhalese and everything, you know. And they hate Tamil people. . . . And our side, they call them Tamil Tigers and because we fight for them. . . . They can't find my uncle anymore and my friend's cousin's uncle found [people] in a cave. . . . Oh, and 2,000 people came on a boat to Canada, and my parents were so happy. One of my cousins was on the boat, too.[7]

In one Grade 8 classroom where I conducted research, a significant number of students were Sri Lankan, and they felt betrayed by Canada's lack of intervention in the war in Sri Lanka. In an interview with a group of Tamil Sri Lankan female students, one stated: "I really *hate* the Canadian government

7 Swetha, whose family was living in Toronto at the time, made these comments in April 2011.

right now," to which her peer replied, "'Cause it's *our* people who're getting affected."[8] As young people acculturate, their allegiance and connection to the country of origin may still be stronger than their connection to Canada. In this particular class, since many students had arrived from high-conflict settings, such as war zones or places where the government was corrupt, their willingness to engage and share perspectives in whole-class discussions was not always easy or welcomed.

Creating a safe space for acculturating students to navigate their cultural identities obviously requires careful planning and preparation of the classroom environment. The multicultural rhetoric of the dominant society has sought to define and normalize our perceptions of difference, but critical pedagogical approaches to issues of diversity can provide students with the autonomy to (re)define their own identities. Dominant narratives or messages about refugees can also influence teachers' practices and responses to different types of children. Guiding students (and teachers) to explore social constructions of race, gender, and privilege, for instance, may also contribute to their increased awareness and understanding of power.

Children do not always want to share their stories. Often, neither do their parents. The trauma, shame, and many deep feelings associated with the refugee process are not something that teachers are necessarily equipped to address; nor should they forcefully address them, even when given the opportunity. Furthermore, for many children awaiting their permanent resident status, focusing on school—or anything else for that matter—becomes challenging.

FACILITATING INCLUSION

In my experience working with immigrant and refugee children, I have found that children often feel more comfortable sharing their story if they feel connected in some way. They may feel connected to a teacher or peer they have aligned with, or to content within the curriculum, or to classroom discussions that closely reflect their experiences. When teachers strive to create an inclusive and safe space for children, the process of building trust and creating an emotionally and physically safe community contributes to helping children heal from trauma.

---

8 This exchange took place in April 2011 at a school in Toronto.

Relationships between students are key indicators of safety in the classroom. Pedagogical tools to facilitate strong and healthy peer relationships are critical for ensuring student safety and inclusion. A Grade 8 teacher, Ms. Rossi, a white female, felt that peacemaking pedagogies such as circle processes (a dialogic pedagogical tool, where students sit in a circle, and use a talking piece to each take turns speaking) were very beneficial for her very transient student population, which included several Syrian, Roma, and Russian students who were refugees. She reflected on how this transient population impacted her role as a teacher:

> I feel like I'm like the maître-d' at a restaurant and I just have to cater to everyone, and people in the neighbourhood are looking on and everyone expects to be accommodated. So I try to make it my business to know everyone's interests in the class, like in a restaurant, which is my classroom, because I want them to be engaged and I want them to feel safe. Since November I have gotten seven new students, who do not all speak English and have various needs, so circles have been really helpful.[9]

One of her newcomer students, a Russian child who did not know much English, was silent for the first two months he was there. Ms. Rossi relied on another Russian student in the class to translate for him. When the child did speak, he often had his head down and turned away. However, during a classroom circle, he spoke for the first time in front of his peers—in English. After he shared, his student peers spontaneously clapped to acknowledge him. In these contexts, the opportunity to speak in well-facilitated circle dialogues seemed over time to encourage more students to participate orally, while also nurturing healthy peer relationships. Ms. Rossi's circle implementation illustrates how, when done effectively, peacemaking pedagogies can increase the opportunities for quieter, English Learner (EL) students to participate orally and feel more included in their classrooms.[10]

Overall, discussing historical conflicts and current events that relate directly to students' lived experiences with conflict can raise further contention

9 Interview with the author, April 21, 2016, Toronto. The teacher's name has been changed for confidentiality.

10 For a detailed account of this incident, see Christina Parker and Kathy Bickmore, "Classroom Peace Circles: Teachers' Professional Learning and Implementation of Restorative Dialogue," *Teaching and Teacher Education* 95 (2020): article 103129.

and, possibly, conflict. Teachers' interpretations and assumptions may impact how or whether they teach about topics that are directly connected to students' experiences. Prior to meeting the students registered in a course I was teaching I planned a lesson that focused on peacebuilding in Sudan. When facilitating this lesson, two students from Sudan raised their hands to contribute to the discussion, offering their own interpretation and sharing their story about coming to Canada as refugees, identifying themselves as Lost Boys of Sudan—orphans who had been separated from their families during attacks in the southern region of Sudan, and who had walked miles to escape war and recruitment as child soldiers. Clearly, my interpretation of this conflict was superseded by these students' experiences. Their willingness to share and educate their peers was also reflective of their trust in their classmates and requisite safety in the classroom necessary to engage in such a difficult conversation.

REFUGEE PARENTS

When parents emigrate with their children, one often hears the phrase "I'm doing this for my children." The *this* often refers to issues ranging from dangerous and risky journeys, to lack of social, cultural, and economic support, and the challenges of integration. Parents often attribute the sacrifice they make in leaving their country of origin, and the strength they develop in overcoming trials and tribulations in immigrating to a completely foreign country, to hope for their children. Still, many teachers are confronted with a wide variance in refugees' parental involvement. In addition to working long hours, refugee parents may not understand how Canadian school systems work. Furthermore, many parents and families are deeply concerned about their child's experience with inclusion and acculturation to their new school community. These concerns vary from fear their child will be rejected to concerns over their child's loss of their own cultural values as they integrate into their new school community.

In many ways, parents of refugee children are further marginalized when they are not met with inclusive and welcoming school personnel. Teachers and school administrators hold a lot of power. The power dynamic between teachers and parents from marginalized backgrounds results in parents becoming passive recipients of information, with little capacity to advocate for their children or even to ask questions. This may be further exacerbated if the parents or guardians do not speak English or lack an understanding of the cultural cues and norms of the dominant society. Strong communication between teachers and parents contributes to children's academic success, but typical strategies for connecting with parents—letters or phone calls—may not always be successful. More successful strategies include access to translators, translated letters home, connecting the new parent to other parents in the school community, and involving parents in activities and events, where they have a special role in the school activity or event. Such efforts help to provide a welcoming and safe forum for refugee parents to engage in their children's schooling. They are also an instrumental factor in preparing for the students' success. When teachers and administrators actively use strategies for supporting communication with refugee parents, the potential for students' success and inclusion heightens.

CONCLUSION

When the needs of refugee children and their families can be met through structural supports embedded in schools, the children will enjoy greater academic success and social and cultural inclusion, and experience a strong pathway facilitating citizenship capacity-building. Encouraging all students, and particularly refugee students and their peers, to identify positively with their classmates, their cultures, and their society is essential for successful integration and inclusion at school. Teachers who are readily equipped with tools and strategies for supporting refugee students' integration and inclusion, and who themselves receive ongoing support, professional development, and adequate resources, can maintain the kind of connection and communication necessary for building strong student communities.

The journey that refugee children experience when coming to Canada, in addition to their age and country of origin, are all factors in determining what kind of support will be effective and useful. Many children who arrive in Canada as refugees have likely experienced violence, trauma, and separation from their family, and they may have been out of school for an extended period of time. Overall, integrating refugee children poses a challenge that teachers and administrators across Canada are facing, particularly when dealing with inadequate resources and supports to contribute to successful integration and acculturation. Without adequate and ongoing support, the outcomes for immigrant and refugee children will be suboptimal at best, and tragic at worst.

What We Know, What We Hope

An Afterword

GEORGE MELNYK *and* CHRISTINA PARKER

As we gathered stories for this collection, we didn't have any particular voices or persons in mind. We sought to connect with people who support refugees, who are refugees, and who work on issues connected to refugees. What we have gathered are stories told from the perspective of those who experienced them first-hand. These perspectives connect to a much larger story about what it means to be a refugee in Canada. The authors speak for themselves with the power of first-hand experience. As co-editors of this book we wanted to emphasize the importance of creating and implementing policies and practices that support human rights in Canada and around the world—protecting persons who face harm is a shared responsibility. These stories offer those of us in positions of power in Canada, as well as those refugees who will surely come to this country in the future, guidance in deciphering the humanness that exists within those classed and identified as refugees. We hope writing their stories for the public has empowered them.

The authors of each chapter approach their understanding of Canada and refugees in their own way; individually and collectively, their perspectives shape how we conceptualize and understand the refugee experience in Canada. These different vantage points provide insight into the lives of refugees in Canada and an awareness of their day-to-day struggles. The wide range of authors illustrates the multifaceted process in which we need to engage when trying to understand refugees' experiences. Some of the authors write from privileged positions, while others continue to occupy marginalized spaces, even in their new home country. Together, their stories illustrate how moving from one physical or psychological space to another does not necessarily erase the initial situations that led to refugees' displacement, but at times merely shifts the location of their liminal existence. Their stories illustrate to what extent individual experiences of forced movement and transition from one space to another are shaped by the specific historical events that frame them.

These stories raise critical questions about the nature of Canada's refugee intake and support system and present important ideas about how the country should engage with refugees. They also point out the flaws in the system. They indicate how Canada uses a mixture of pragmatism and humanitarianism to justify its refugee policies over time. They highlight the human cost of being a refugee. The stories in this volume lay the groundwork for necessary, yet difficult, conversations about how to integrate refugees in Canada. Some of the backlash we see against refugees is based on xenophobia and racism and exaggerated security concerns. Some of it is rooted in ignorance of the legal obligations that Canada has to asylum seekers. Yet more of it is fanned by political rhetoric about "queue jumping." These stories are meant to move the discussion from the realm of politically loaded terminology toward a space that is respectful of the human experience.

The global pandemic has, unfortunately, exacerbated the marginal status of already disadvantaged groups. News reports indicate that COVID-19 has had a disproportionately harmful impact on these groups in terms of both economic welfare and health (including personal well-being and access to medical care). We in Canada are witnessing a widening gap in how this nation responds to the need for safety and protection of dominant as opposed to marginalized groups, with the latter bearing the brunt of the difference. This trend toward the prioritization of the haves over the have-nots—of insiders over outsiders—has a direct impact on refugees. In the climate of fear and mutual mistrust that the pandemic has created, our human capacity to respond with compassion to the needs of others is temporarily diminished. This, in turn, erodes Canadians' sense of themselves as members of an inclusive community that is prepared to welcome refugees.

Our hope for this collection is to deepen and broaden the network that supports refugees and to illustrate refugees' personal activism and abilities to speak their truth to power and in doing so reach more decision makers with the ultimate goal of making real change in the lives of refugees. As this collection illustrates, refugees and those who support refugees engage in an acculturation process that develops the civic competencies needed for success in a diverse workforce and pluralistic society. While COVID-19 has compromised this process of integration and inclusion—severely impacting the protection and welfare of those in most need of shelter and protection—it is our hope that Canada can become a leader in securing the protection of those most vulnerable during this global crisis.

VOICE AND POWER IN REFUGEE NARRATIVES

As Chimamanda Ngozi Adichie points out in "The Danger of a Single Story," her TED talk about the power of storytelling, "It is impossible to talk about the single story without talking about power. . . . Power is the ability not just to tell the story of another person, but to make it the definitive story of that person."[1] In other words, the "single" dominant narrative of refugees happily arriving and settling in Canada is challenged through the voices represented in this collection. They indicate the trials and tribulations of the migratory experience and the real and sometimes overwhelming challenges of adapting to a new life in a strange new place. The idea of a benign and generous Canada that is open to helping others through resettlement must be tempered by the individual experiences of refugees who have to deal with so many issues and emotions, including guilt for leaving behind relatives and loved ones, and the effort to maintain a dignified identity in a sometimes hostile environment. While some of the experiences that are related in this collection are transferable and connect to the experiences of others, each narrative remains an account of a unique experience of resettlement and integration. By letting these individual stories stand alongside each other to reflect a multifaceted experience of forced migration, this collection helps to give refugees, and those involved in assisting them, a voice. That itself is an act of affirmation, as Adichie points out.

It is not uncommon for refugees to fear telling their story. This may be because they fear that colleagues or family members in their home country

---

1 Chimamanda Ngozi Adichie, "The Danger of a Single Story," TEDGlobal, July 2009, https://www.ted.com/talks/chimamanda_ngozi_adichie_the_danger_of_a_ single_story?language=en.

or in the diaspora may be persecuted if they tell these stories. In hearing these stories, we become aware of how precarious their sense of security still is, especially those who are recent newcomers. Their past experiences of persecution haunt them still. This fear is not unfounded. When refugees arrive in Canada, they are powerless. They are without a home and are often still awaiting status. The process of determining their future could take years. Those who are dependent on government aid or on private sponsorship support and have to survive without resources of their own are often left voiceless; they are spoken to, and some speak on behalf of them, but too often they do not, or feel they cannot, speak for themselves. Giving these people the space to tell their stories inverts these power relations and allows us to see how refugees' lives are still defined by the will of those who have power.

The stories represented in this book invite us to reflect critically on the policies and practices that are necessary to drive the kind of transformation that is needed that will support refugees in their efforts to reclaim their voices. Their stories invite us to ask if there are processes that should be implemented in the refugee determination process that would make refugees active participants in the design of their future lives. We need to ask ourselves how we might encourage those seeking refuge in Canada to participate in developing the policies that affect them. While the refugee determination process has many elements that seem to make sense from the perspective of protecting the country from bogus applications, and thereby ensuring the integrity of the immigration process, there is no reason why the system cannot be upgraded and reformed into a more equitable process for all concerned. These first-person accounts allow us to reflect on the ways in which various communities, contexts, and cultures shape the refugee determination process and its outcomes. The moral and existential dilemmas the authors in this volume have faced, and continue to face, as refugees should serve as the basis of any authentic re-examination of the refugee process.

HUMANIZING REFUGEES: WHAT WE'VE LEARNED

Over the decades, Canada has variously invited refugees into the house or turned them away, as George Melnyk shows in his contribution to this volume. Sometimes government responses have emphasized humanitarian considerations, while at other times Canada has reacted with exclusionary policies that spark conflict and criticism. Refugee workers such as Eusebio Garcia and Shelley Campagnola do their best to help asylum seekers navigate the bureaucratic processes of a cumbersome system that may, or may not, eventually allow them to remain in Canada—the country where, by the time a decision is made, they may already have lived for several years. Because of bureaucratic delays, private sponsors like Katharine Lake Berz and Julia Holland are sometimes left in limbo waiting for a family to support. As they also discovered, refugees—while relieved to no longer be in limbo themselves—live with fears, sorrows, and regrets, even as they are abruptly plunged into a radically unfamiliar culture.

The key issue facing any refugee is the process of settling in their new home. Their perceptions of identity and belonging shape how they negotiate new ways of bridging and connecting their experiences. Their identities are in a process of transformation, and conflicts may never be resolved. Identity may be socially constructed, but it is not a singular construct; it is multiple and fluid. It shifts in response to social contexts, yet it also reflects a person's cultural heritage, which persists but is recontextualized when they move from one national setting to another. We see this process of bridging old and new in Boban Stojanović's story. His experiences with persecution in Serbia deeply influence his connection to his new Canadian identity, but they also continue to fuel his gay activist identity.

What we have learned throughout the stories in this book is that is takes a great deal of courage to make the journey to a foreign place as a refugee. Each refugee moves with their own story, yet their courageous actions move with them. Their courage is further tested as they attempt to integrate in their new home, all apparently with varying levels of support. The Hassan family made their courageous journey from Syria, and their connection to their private sponsors has provided them with a strong support system. As a refugee settlement worker, Garcia frequents the Immigration Holding Centre, where he visits with those detained when attempting to enter Canada. Those detained at point of entry do not always have their claims approved, and many are deported, as they lack the resources and justification to support their claim. Clearly, there are some refugees who experience a high level of support and others who are not as fortunate. Many assumptions and responses to refugees are skewed by misperceptions based on the identities of those claiming refugee status. Their identities including gender, class, race, religion, or literacy level, impact their experience and subsequent outcomes. Pablo Policzer closes his essay with a reflection on the processes used to screen refugees. "At some point in the future, perhaps, refugees may be able to become citizens without continually demonstrating their victim-hood," he writes. This would be a significant development, as victimhood is something most refugees would like to put behind them.

The outcomes for refugees in Canada vary just as much as the levels of support refugees receive. Refugees are faced with internal and external obligations of doing good and being good. Victor Porter's arrival in Canada in the 1980s, after experiencing torture during his four years as a political prisoner in Argentina, was marked with further challenges, as he learned how to speak English and to integrate while working in minimum-wage jobs to build a new life. Matida Daffeh continues to pursue her studies, despite her ongoing fears about her past and future. Despite the many integration challenges that refugees face, they are still burdened with the expectation to "do good and be good." In exchange for their chance at a new life in Canada, they are expected to carry gratitude with them forever and be exemplary residents.

All the same, those seeking refuge in Canada are full of hope. They wish to find a reason to be thankful. The voices represented in this book speak to the truths, triumphs, and tribulations of coming to Canada and resettling in a new home. These stories—the hope and resilience embedded in each— must allow us to gain the courage necessary to participate in the struggle for the ongoing support of people who have sought refuge in Canada. In 2016, when Justin Trudeau formally apologized on behalf of the Canadian people for refusing entry to the passengers on the *Komagata Maru* more than a century earlier, he said: "When we have the choice between opening our arms to those in need or closing our hearts to them, we must always choose the more compassionate path." It is a fitting reminder with which to end.

About the Authors

Howard Adelman, professor emeritus of philosophy at York University, published his last two books in 2011: *No Return, No Refuge* (co-author Elazar Barkan) with Columbia University Press and *Religion, Culture and the State* (co-editor Pierre Anctil) with the University of Toronto Press. Adelman, the founding director of the Centre for Refugee Studies and editor of *Refuge* until 1993, has written or co-authored eight books, edited or co-edited nineteen others and authored over two hundred scholarly papers in book chapters and academic journals. He has continued to write articles, but his main efforts are now invested in a blog that can be read on Word Press under Howard Adelman.

Shelley Campagnola is the director of the Mennonite Coalition for Refugee Support (MCRS). She has had long career working with people of all ages in a variety of business, charitable, and not-for-profit contexts in local, national, and international settings. Her strengths are in organizational realignment, strategic planning and program development, research and leadership development, and community partnerships and integration. Since May 2016, when Campagnola joined MCRS, there have been significant changes globally, politically, socially, and economically pertaining to refugee claimants. She has increasingly been one of the many leaders on the cutting edge speaking about ways that communities and organizations can respond to ensure welcome, compassion, inclusion, and justice for people seeking refuge.

Matida Daffeh, anti-female genital mutilation and feminist activist from Republic of The Gambia, West Africa, is the co-founder of The Girls Agenda, a grassroots feminist movement working to end FGM and other traditional practices that violate the rights of women and girls. Daffeh has over ten years of experience working in both non-governmental and community-based organizations (at national and sub-regional levels) in the field of women's empowerment, including promoting the leadership and political participation of women, and issues related to gender-based violence among others.

Eusebio Garcia is a refugee and settlement worker with the Quaker Committee for Refugees. Garcia assists refugees and other migrants through Friends House Toronto to file forms, apply for work permits, access health care coverage, obtain necessary documents, connect to legal services, find housing, understand educational options and openings, receive employment training, and more.

Julia Holland is a lawyer and director at Tory's LLP, where she is responsible for risk management across the firm. Prior to assuming responsibility for risk management, Julia practiced litigation at Tory's for ten years. Julia has a Bachelor of Arts from Harvard University and an LLM from the University of Toronto.

William Janzen grew up in Saskatchewan but has spent most of his adult life in Ottawa, where he served as director of the Ottawa office of the Mennonite Central Committee (MCC) from 1975 to 2008. In this capacity he did advocacy work on a range of domestic and international issues while also representing MCC on various ecumenical and other coalitions such as Project Ploughshares. He has travelled to many parts of the world and lived in the Congo and in Egypt—spending approximately two years in each country. His education includes a PhD in political science from Carleton University and MA degrees in international affairs and in religion from Carleton and the University of Ottawa. He is married and has two adult children.

Katharine Lake Berz is an independent consultant and writer living in Toronto. Katharine was a management consultant at McKinsey & Company for ten years and has since advised a number of not-for-profit organizations. Recently Katharine helped establish a centre for launching new social enterprises and supporting research and communications for a public policy institute. Katharine has held board of director roles for five community organizations including one that helped settle twenty Syrian refugee families.

Katharine holds a Bachelor of Commerce from Queen's University and a Master of Philosophy in International Relations from Cambridge University.

George Melnyk is professor emeritus of communication, media, and film at the University of Calgary. He is a cultural historian who is the author or editor of twenty-five books, primarily on Canadian topics. He came to Canada as a stateless child-refugee with his parents. He was educated at the Universities of Manitoba, Chicago, and Toronto. He maintains a website of his most recent writings at www.georgemelnyk.com.

Michael Molloy joined the immigration foreign service in 1968 and served in Tokyo, Beirut, Kampala, and Minneapolis before returning to Ottawa in 1976 where he was director, refugee policy. As such, he led the design of the refugee provisions of the 1976 Immigration Act, including the Convention Refugee and Designated Classes and the private refugee sponsorship program. He was senior coordinator of the 1979–80 Indochinese refugee program that brought 60,000 refugees to Canada. He served as counsellor for humanitarian affairs at the Canadian Mission in Geneva and managed immigration and refugee operations in Jordan, Syria, and East Africa. After director-general level assignments in Ottawa and Toronto, he served as Canada's ambassador to Jordan (1996–2000) and special coordinator for the Middle East Peace Process (2000–3). An adjunct professor at the University of Ottawa's Graduate School of Public and International Affairs, he is co-director of the Jerusalem Old City Initiative and president of the Canadian Immigration Historical Society.

Christina Parker is an assistant professor in social development studies at Renison University College at the University of Waterloo. She holds a PhD and a master's in teaching from the Ontario Institute for Studies in Education (OISE) of the University of Toronto and is an Ontario Certified Teacher, with a specialization in teaching history. Parker's research on peacebuilding education in diverse multicultural classrooms with immigrant and refugee children shows how dialogic pedagogies facilitate inclusive spaces where all students can participate and have their voices heard. She is the author of *Peacebuilding, Citizenship, and Identity: Empowering Conflict and Dialogue in Multicultural Elementary Classrooms* (Brill | Sense, 2016).

Adam Policzer and **Irene Boisier** met when they studied architecture in Santiago's Universidad de Chile. They married and had three children. They were active supporters of Salvador Allende's government. In 1973, the government was overthrown by a military coup. Adam was imprisoned for two years. When he was freed, the family came to Canada. After validating his credentials, Adam opened a private architectural practice, specializing in social housing. Irene, after receiving a master's in urban planning at the University of British Columbia, worked as a city planner and later as a community development worker helping marginalized people, mostly immigrants and refugees. At present they are both retired, living in Vancouver.

Pablo Policzer is an associate professor of political science at the University of Calgary. A specialist in comparative politics, his research focuses on the evolution of violent conflict in authoritarian and democratic regimes. His book *The Rise and Fall of Repression in Chile* (Notre Dame University Press, 2009) won the 2010 award for best book in comparative politics from the Canadian Political Science Association. He obtained his PhD in political science from the Massachusetts Institute of Technology and his BA (Honours, First Class) in political science from the University of British Columbia.

Victor Porter is originally from Buenos Aires, Argentina. He arrived in Vancouver in 1984 as a government-assisted refugee. He has worked in a variety of jobs: dishwasher, cook, beekeeper, production line worker, advocate, popular education facilitator, coordinating British Columbia's response to human trafficking, and recently as a negotiator with the Hospital Employees Union. He lives with his wife, Maria Inés. They have four children—Maria Teresa, Paula Isabel, Camilo, and Jorge Luis.

Cyrus Sundar Singh is an AcademiCreActivist: Gemini Award–winning filmmaker, doctoral scholar, and musician, as well as a poet and storyteller. His recent installation *Emancipation2Africville* formed part of the Africville: Reflection Project at the MSVU Art Gallery in Nova Scotia (2019), and his mobile phone installation *footage*, an homage to Bata Shoe Museum, was installed at the 2018 WC2 Symposium, held at Ryerson University, in Toronto. His directorial debut, *Film Club*, is the winner of both a Gemini Award and the National Film Board of Canada's Reel Diversity Award. On the foundation of his sixteen-year documentary career, he conceived and successfully explored a new site-specific hybrid live documentary genre,

Performing the Documentary, with world premieres at Hot Docs Canadian International Documentary Festival—*Brothers in the Kitchen* (2016), *Africville in Black and White* (2017)—and at the Atlantic Film Festival (2018).

Boban Stojanović is a Serbian-Canadian peace and human rights activist who now lives in Calgary, where he works as a settlement practitioner and outreach worker for LGBTQ+ Services at the Centre for Newcomers. He was a founder and one of the key organizers of the Belgrade Pride Parade. In 2013, Stojanović was the first gay person to participate in the Serbian edition of Celebrity Big Brother. In the same year, he published his autobiography *As If Everything Was OK*. He was International Grand Marshal at Montréal Pride 2014. A year later he was shortlisted as one of the top five LGBTQ+ activists in the world (David Kato—Vision and Voice Award).

Flora Terah is a Kenyan Canadian author, a public speaker, and the ambassador for ShelterBox Canada. Trained as a social worker, she has a wealth of experience as an HIV/AIDS trainer and women's rights advocate in her native country of Kenya as well as in her adopted home of Canada. As a victim of horrible violent acts, the need for peaceful solutions is never far from her thoughts. She has combined her experience as grassroots organizer, educator, and women's rights defender with her experience as a survivor of violence to become a powerful role model for non-violence in Canada and around the world. Since arriving in Canada in 2009, Terah has been active in several Canadian organizations, sharing her expertise and participating in public education campaigns on the violence that women and children face. She has continued this advocacy with the Stephen Lewis Foundation, Jean Sauvé Foundation, McGill University, York University, Carleton University, and Canadian Lawyers Abroad, among others. A lot of what she has done is deemed motivational and supports her desire to end the violence and bullying experienced by women and children, thus creating peaceful environments locally and beyond borders.